£3·95

82 N

TEXT AND PERFORMANCE

General Editor: Michael Scott

The series is designed to introduce sixth-form and undergraduate students to the themes, continuing vitality and performance of major dramatic works. The attention given to production aspects is an element of special importance, responding to the invigoration given to literary study by the work of leading contemporary critics.

The prime aim is to present each play as a vital experience in the mind of the reader – achieved by analysis of the text in relation to its themes and theatricality. Emphasis is accordingly placed on the relevance of the work to the modern reader and the world of today. At the same time, traditional views are presented and appraised, forming the basis from which a creative response to the text can develop.

In each volume, Part One: *Text* discusses certain key themes or problems, the reader being encouraged to gain a stronger perception both of the inherent character of the work and also of variations in interpreting it. Part Two: *Performance* examines the ways in which these themes or problems have been handled in modern productions, and the approaches and techniques employed to enhance the play's accessibility to modern audiences.

A synopsis of the play is given and an outline of its major sources, and a concluding Reading List offers guidance to the student's independent study of the work.

PUBLISHED

IN PREPARATION

VOLPONE

Text and Performance

ARNOLD P. HINCHLIFFE

MACMILLAN

First published 1985

Published by
Higher and Further Education Division
MACMILLAN PUBLISHERS LTD
Houndmills, Basingstoke, Hampshire RG21 2XS
and London
Companies and representatives throughout the world.

Typeset by
Wessex Typesetters Ltd
Frome, Somerset

Printed in Hong Kong

British Library Cataloguing in Publication Data
Hinchliffe, Arnold P.
Volpone. – (Text and performance)
1. Jonson, Ben. *Volpone*
I. Title   II. Series
822′.3   PR2622
ISBN 0–333–34312–3

CONTENTS

Illustrations will be found in Part Two

ACKNOWLEDGEMENTS

Quotations from the text of the play are from the New Mermaid edition (1968), edited by J. P. Brockbank. Source-details for the illustrations are given with the relevant captions.

I have tried to record my debts to other Jonson critics in the text and the Reading List, but in a work of this kind there are other forms of indebtedness. I should like to thank Miss Alex Stockwell at the National Theatre, Dr Levi Fox and his staff at the Shakespeare Birthplace Trust, Stratford-upon-Avon, and the staff at Colindale, at the Theatre Museum of the Victoria and Albert Museum, at the National Portrait Gallery and at the Harvard Theater Collection, for their co-operation. Individual colleagues and specialists, too, have helped me enormously, and I should like to thank Desmond Green, Ronald Harwood, David Hirst, Roger Holdsworth, Angus McBean, Giovanni Pontiero, Tony Simlick and Reg Wilson. Finally, I must thank the series editor, Michael Scott, Penny who did the typing, and Jim who listened.

A.P.H.

NOTE ON PLOT SYNOPSIS

In this volume in the series, an outline of the plot is integral to the text, and will be found in section 4 ('The Double Plot') of Part One, especially on pages 27–9.

GENERAL EDITOR'S PREFACE

For many years a mutual suspicion existed between the theatre director and the literary critic of drama. Although in the first half of the century there were important exceptions, such was the rule. A radical change of attitude, however, has taken place over the last thirty years. Critics and directors now increasingly recognise the significance of each other's work and acknowledge their growing awareness of interdependence. Both interpret the same text, but do so according to their different situations and functions. Without the director, the designer and the actor, a play's existence is only partial. They revitalise the text with action, enabling the drama to live fully at each performance. The academic critic investigates the script to elucidate its textual problems, understand its conventions and discover how it operates. He may also propose his view of the work, expounding what he considers to be its significance.

Dramatic texts belong therefore to theatre and to literature. The aim of the 'Text and Performance' series is to achieve a fuller recognition of how both enhance our enjoyment of the play. Each volume follows the same basic pattern. Part One provides a critical introduction to the play under discussion, using the techniques and criteria of the literary critic in examining the manner in which the work operates through language, imagery and action. Part Two takes the enquiry further into the play's theatricality by focusing on selected productions of recent times so as to illustrate points of contrast and comparison in the interpretation of different directors and actors, and to demonstrate how the drama has worked on the modern stage. In this way the series seeks to provide a lively and informative introduction to major plays in their text and performance.

MICHAEL SCOTT

PART ONE: TEXT

1 INTRODUCTION

Jonson marked a new scene whenever the entry or exit of a character changed the focus of interest. This, the classical or French system, is used by most editors. References to the text here follow Brockbank's edition which uses this system. Some editors, however – for example, David Cook – prefer the modern English system. In this latter convention Act I, for example, has only one scene instead of five as in Jonson's own organisation of the text.

The plot of *Volpone* is original. As Alvin B. Kernan points out in the Yale edition of the play, Jonson began with an idea where Shakespeare began with a story; Jonson then illustrated that idea from his wide-ranging scholarship. Thus, though it has no specific source, *Volpone* draws on the literature and drama of the past. The idea of legacy-hunting, for example, can be found in Horace and Lucian and Petronius, and the play contains echoes of the Bible, Aesop's Fables, Aristophanes, Juvenal, Tacitus and Erasmus – to name but a few obvious connections.

2 RARE BEN

Hazlitt* tried hard to like Jonson but found his power repulsive and unamiable. Tennyson could not read him because he appeared to move 'in a wide sea of glue'. Bernard Shaw called him a brutal pedant, while Edmund Wilson characterised the author of *Volpone* as an anal erotic. Coleridge* dubbed him a mammoth or megatherium; Taine, and later Arthur Symons, saw him as a Spanish galleon (while Shakespeare was an English man-o'-war). William Archer likened him to the pyramids, the Tower of London, and a tank. (A tank – or a galleon, for that matter – is, of course, slow, bulky and

---

* Authors and critics signalised by an asterisk, as here, will be found excerpted in the Casebook on *Volpone*, edited by Jonas A. Barish.

mechanical: all of which suits a dramatist whose characters are puppets.) T. S. Eliot* expresses the problem perfectly: Ben Jonson has an immense reputation and his work excites admiration, but gives little pleasure. The weight of his learning damns the tragedies and, by implication, the comedies too. He is a difficult poet, one who requires study, who needs an 'intelligent saturation in his work as a whole'. He is a man of his times (and so we must study those times) whereas Shakespeare is a man for all times. It is ironic that Jonson's own description of Shakespeare ('He was not for an age but for all time') should so often be used against himself. And so we have a Royal Shakespeare Company but not – as Terry Hands remarks – a Republican Jonson Theatre.

Ben Johnson – the spelling 'Jonson' was his own choice – was born in 1572/73 shortly after the death of his father, a minister. He was educated at Westminster School, then a grammar school for local boys, with forty free scholarships. Here he was taught by William Camden, then in his late twenties but already showing promise as the great antiquarian scholar he later became. From Camden, Jonson learned to respect the classics, and also – unusual for the time in schoolrooms – to recognise the dignity and value of poetry. His education at Westminster took him as far as it could, but he went to neither of the universities, since his stepfather had him bound apprentice to his own trade of bricklaying. Ben served as a soldier in the Low Countries (he was probably conscripted) and on his return he married, although he had not yet completed his seven years' apprenticeship. Of his wife we know only that she was said by her husband, to be 'a shrew yet honest'. Jonson did not return to bricklaying: he became an actor and writer.

In 1597 he joined the company at Frederick Langley's new theatre, The Swan (set up in competition with the Chamberlain's Company – of which Shakespeare was a member – and the Admiral's Company). Langley in the same year put on *The Isle of Dogs*, written by Thomas Nashe and Ben Jonson. This the Privy Council declared subversive and imprisoned members of the company, including Jonson. There was a great risk that the scandal over the play would lead to the permanent closing of all London's theatres but this fortunately did not come about; instead a new licensing system was devised to control performances in the capital. Langley's Swan, however, was refused a licence and Jonson, on his release, joined the Admiral's Company at The Rose, managed by Philip Henslowe. Here he was employed as a playwright rather than as an actor.

This was not to be Jonson's sole acquaintance with the penal system. In the following year (1598) he was indicted for killing an actor in a duel. He would almost certainly have suffered the penalty for murder had he not been able to plead 'benefit of clergy'. This survival of a medieval legal provision, designed to protect men in holy orders (the only persons, in an earlier age, who could read) made it possible for Jonson – by showing that he could read aloud a passage from the Psalter – to escape the capital charge; and after a period in prison he emerged a free man. (For the rest of his life he bore a mark on his left thumb, branded there to prevent any subsequent 'benefit of clergy' plea.) Seven years later, in 1605, he was again imprisoned, in connection with the play *Eastward Hoe* (a collaborative venture with George Chapman and John Marston) which the authorities judged offensive in its mockery of the Scots (an ill-judged exercise of wit, with a Stuart now on the throne of England!).

Although in later life much revered for his paternal interest in young writers, among his peers and rivals in his earlier career Jonson had a reputation for pugnacity and vehemence: characteristics stemming both from his inherent personality and also from his strong and reasoned revulsion against what he judged to be the low standards and stylistic extravagance of much of the play-writing of his day. He was, for example, a major combatant in the 'War of the Theatres' of 1599–1601, engaged most notably against Thomas Dekker and John Marston. Each side produced plays attacking the style and dramatic pretensions of the other. The main interest of the 'war' for us is in its stimulating Jonson to write *Every Man out of his Humour* (1599), the first of what he called his 'comic satires'. Another of his war-weapons was *The Poetaster* (1601). Here Johnson pushed the battleline beyond theatrical objectives, satirising influential men. Danger loomed again for him. He withdrew from the risky ground of comedy for a time, and set to work on a tragedy, *Sejanus*. (Interestingly, the war, though fought very briskly,

produced no lasting rift among the contending dramatists; and
it certainly filled the theatres!)

We have then a picture of an energetic, passionate – even
quarrelsome – man; also a man of determination and a
reformer. A colourful character, his literary career lasted for
some forty years: much longer than any of his contemporaries.
He had a firm sense of his own role in the craft of letters. Hazlitt
complains of Jonson's overweening admiration for his own
works; and indeed he does, like Shaw, harangue us tirelessly
with Prefaces, Prologues and Epilogues. It is characteristic that
it should be *his* works that achieved the status of the first
'collected edition' in the history of English publishing – the
1616 Folio volume containing verses and some of his plays,
issued under Jonson's own title of *The Works of Ben Jonson*. (A
revised edition, in two volumes, was published in 1640, three
years after the author's death). There was more to this
publication than Jonson's argument that the theatre would not
be taken seriously until it began to look after its playscripts. A
royal pension in 1616 made him Poet Laureate, in fact if not in
name, and in the *Works* volume he assembled a miscellany of
plays, poems and masques to sum up his whole career. By
printing playscripts along with poems in the same volume, he
redefined the significance of the drama text – thus preparing
the way for the Shakespearean First Folio of 1623 and the
publication of many Jacobean plays that might otherwise have
been lost. But essentially the *Works* volume's intention was to
commemorate the laureateship.

It says much for the 'official' temper of the period that royal
patronage of this kind should be given to a writer who earlier
had so notably fallen foul of the authorities. But Jonson, despite
his 'record', enjoyed a favoured position in court circles. James I's
accession in 1603 introduced an era of masques and regal
entertainments, the first of which was the commission from the
queen (Anne of Denmark) for Jonson to create, in 1604, a
Christmas masque in which she and her ladies could appear (as
blackamoors!). In the production of this first court masque by
Jonson use was made of an arch draped across its width by a
large curtain, concealing the set from the audience until the
moment the performance began – perhaps the first instance in

England of the 'proscenium arch'. The set was designed by
Inigo Jones, who had been trained in Italy. For twenty years
Jonson produced masques for the court, often in collaboration
with Jones. The equivalent for the modern dramatist would be
film work.

His major work, however, from the outset of his career and
thereafter, was for the popular theatre. *Every Man in his Humour*
– performed in 1598 at The Curtain by the Chamberlain's Men
(including Shakespeare) and dedicated to William Camden –
was an immediate success. Jonson offered it as a model towards
which the theatre should move, and in its preface set out the
manifesto of a playwright who had found a different way of
doing things from his peers (including Shakespeare). He rejects
the loosely structured chronicle history play in favour of a
drama that abides by 'the Unities', dismissing the 'creaking
throne' and the 'tempestuous drum' of romantic theatre for the
deeds and language of men. Members of the audience are not to
be taken out of themselves; they are to be held by the
truthfulness of the action in which the dramatist will examine
what human beings do and have done to them: the governing
aim being understanding, not suspension of disbelief. Thus, the
location – fixed in the original version in a rather vague
Florence – is that of a very specific London, with language and
atmosphere to match. Yet *Every Man in his Humour* does not – as
do Jonson's best comedies – cause self-examination. The
machinating servant Brainworm is still too much a plot-
contriver of a conventional kind (a puppet animated to
manipulate other puppets); and the kindly figure of Judge
Clement is too patently a manufactured instrument for achieving the happy ending which the audience can applaud without
much concern for their own involvement in the issues raised by
the play. This early success also fixed on Jonson the 'Humours'
label, which has too greatly engrossed critical attention.

For this the dramatist has only himself to blame, for he called
his next play (of 1559, one of his forrays in the 'War of the
Theatres') *Every Man out of his Humour*. Despite its title, this was
not a sequel to the previous play; it was, as Jonson himself
admitted, a thing 'strange, and of a particular kind by itself'.
Less amusing and more censorious, this first of Jonson's 'comic
satires' (his own term) presents characters who may or may not

be fellow dramatists. If they are such, they are also *typical*, standing for those deformities of the times which their creator declared he would 'anatomise in every nerve, and sinew'. But here also he treats only of the affection of humour, whereas his best comedies deal with real humours. In *Volpone* he will show us characters who have problems – men who are so much in love with themselves that they have lost touch with the real world and with their responsibilities as human beings.

As noted earlier, Jonson in 1601 warily withdrew for a time from writing comedies. Under the patronage of Sir Robert Townshend, and later of Lord Aubigny, he set to work on *Sejanus His Fall* (produced in 1603 at The Globe). Having set a model for comedy in *Every Man in his Humour*, so with *Sejanus* he determined to give the English stage a truly classical tragedy: a model to rectify what he found faulty in the handling of tragic themes in the contemporary theatre. His reverence for the classic tradition led him to re-create rather than imitate. *Sejanus* is a very historical play, and in its subsequent printed version (1605) Jonson cited in the margins all the relevant sources from Latin authors, to demonstrate his adherence to the principle that tragedy, to be effective, must be based on historical fact. If the form is not absolutely faithful to classical rules (there is no Chorus, and the Unity of Time is not observed), its contents are – though Jonson appears to have used his sources very imaginatively! Sejanus himself is a sly Machiavel rather than the blunt, albeit ambitious, soldier portrayed by Tacitus; while Emperor Tiberius becomes the absolute Machiavel who triumphs in the end. The moral is clear and (for the con-temporary audience) orthodox: God punishes those who plot against even the worst of princes. The special interest for us, in connection with *Volpone*, lies in Jonson's depiction of virtue opposed to evil (the latter represented, in different forms, by Tiberius, Sejanus, Macro and Caligula). The men of virtue – followers of Germanicus and their spokesman, Arruntius – are inactive. The dramatist seems to be prompting us to ask how good men should behave in such a confrontation. It appears he is suggesting that merely being pious is not enough. The audience (presumed to be virtuous) are being required to consider what *they* would have done.

This looks forward to the virtuous characters in *Volpone*

where, after Bonario has intervened, Celia and he simply stand
back and appeal to Heaven – in the outcome praising Heaven
for a dénouement in which it played no part. The virtuous are
saved because knaves fall out! In its construction *Sejanus* is
better than anything Jonson had written previously. Obedi-
ence to the Unity of Time in the early plays had served only to
hold the material within conventional forms. Here in his first
tragedy – though it covers more than the twenty-four hours
prescribed by classical convention – there is a strong sense of
movement in the drama, gathering momentum from act to act.
This structure was to serve him well in *Volpone*.

Sejanus was not, however, immediately followed by another
play in tragic form. Jonson in the next couple of years was
engaged in various royal entertainments and with the co-
authored, prisonward-propelling production of *Eastward Hoe*. In
that same year (1605) the printed version of *Sejanus* appeared.
This differed from the text of the stage version of 1603 in more
than its learned annotations. For *Sejanus*, in its turn, had proved a
'dangerous' play in performance – the Earl of Northampton, for
one, charging its author with 'popery and treason' (to add to
the complication, Jonson had had a brawl with one of the earl's
followers!). Prudence recommended a change of genre once
more, it seems, and Jonson returned to comedy.

In five weeks during the winter of 1605–6 he wrote *Volpone*. It
was performed in 1606 by Shakespeare's company at The
Globe, and later in the year (or in 1607) it was staged for
university audiences at Cambridge and Oxford. Its printed text
was issued in Quarto in 1607, and later in the first volume of the
Works (1616).

Jonson had relatively few examples of classic comedy to
follow – chiefly the plays of Plautus and Terence who had
naturalised for the Roman theatre the comedy of manners
developed by late Greek dramatists – but he had more than
enough rules and regulations to take cognizance of. There were
Aristotle and Horace, each of whom would have been very
surprised to learn that he had laid down rules for the writing of
plays! There was also – among many other authorities – the
work of the great literary theorist, Julius Caesar Scaliger
(1484–1558). It was probably Sir Philip Sidney – in *An Apologie*

for Poetrie (privately circulated in manuscript after c. 1580 and printed in 1595, after the poet's death) – who gave Jonson the encouragement to essay a higher flight in his work, by recalling that a poet, if despised in present times, had been a priest and philosopher held in honour in ancient days. Certainly Jonson follows Sidney in his *Timber; or Discoveries Made upon Men and Matter* (posthumously published in the revised edition of *Works*, in 1640). Here his random thoughts about writing – whether intended as notes for lectures given at Gresham College, or made simply as comments in his commonplace book – cover the ground of his ideas better than his more formal statements. Jonson followed 'the rules' more closely than Shakespeare did, but a dislike of arbitrary injunctions saved him from pedantry and 'untheatricality'. Nothing, he observers, is more ridiculous than to make Aristotle a dictator.

The action of *Volpone* occurs in a single day, not because Aristotle so ruled in his *Poetics*, but because Jonson needed the compression to give his action speed and inevitability. Elements in the play are certainly drawn from Greek and Roman literature, but it is also a realistic and original drama. Its author found the contemporary English theatre unrealistic, sensational and untidy, and he wished to wean his audience away from fantasy to fact, from monsters to men. The true dramatist, Jonson wrote, 'will not run away from nature, as he were afraid of her; or depart from life, and the likeness of Truth'. He rejects the Tamburlaines and Tamer-Chams which have nothing but 'scenicall strutting, and furious vociferation, to warrant them to the ignorant gapers'. He concedes (and the course of his reputation among critics confirms this) that his way will get him called 'barren, dull, leane, a poor Writer . . .'.

Jonson himself was the first serious critic of *Volpone* when he anticipated, in the dedicatory epistle, one of the main problems of the play: the ending. Here, as usual, he is concerned with the true poet's mission ('to inform men in the best reason of living') and the need to reform the stage from its present deplorable state. It needs to be said, however, that the deplorable stage at this time was putting on such plays as *King Lear* and *Antony and Cleopatra*! Jonson admits that he has not been able to give us the expected happy ending to his play. The five criminals have been imprisoned in the shapes they have chosen; Mosca is a

galley slave, Volpone will be crippled in a way that matches his
moral nature, Voltore is exiled from the profession he has
debased, Corbaccio is confined to a monastery where he can
remember that he has a soul, and Corvino is turned into a
public joke, pilloried, wearing an ass's cap. The judicial court
that sentences them has been shown as gullible and venal. The
two other principal characters of the unadmirable sort are sent
away. Of the virtuous pair, Celia has her dowry trebled
(presumably for another marriage) and Bonario gets his
inheritance. But theirs is the only 'happy' element in the
ending.

The end of comedy, Jonson suggests, is not always joyful. He
could appeal to Sidney who argued that those who insist upon
laughter as the end of comedy are wrong, and to Aristotle who
had described laughter as 'a fault in Comedy'. Dryden, later,
agreed and suggested that laughter was only accidental. But
the popular idea of comedy consists of two simple notions: if a
play makes you laugh it is a comedy, and a play with a happy
ending must be a comedy. Both may be unreliable criteria (and
vague) but they cannot lightly be dismissed. Shakespeare's
comedies usually do end joyously, and with a wedding or two;
yet, as Eric Bentley observes (*The Life of the Drama*, 1965)

> there is nothing cynical about the happy endings of Shakespeare's
> romantic comedies, but the non-cynicism is childlike: we are not
> asked to apply the formula to marriages outside the world of the
> play. In less 'romantic' comedy, there is the more definite
> implication of: But this is what does *not* happen in life. When we
> read the last act of *Volpone*, we know we are seeing life, not as it is,
> but as it ought to be. Art is normative, and leads Ben Jonson to this
> form of happy ending: the punishment of the wicked.

This is realism again. Jonson asks the audience whether they
want their dreams fulfilled in a happy ending in spite of the
contents of the play. Or do they, like the clients, turn spiteful
when they are disabused of their dream of a happy ending? The
epilogue specifically asks them to rise above that.

No other dramatist, surely, has been criticised as much for
not being Shakespeare. John Dryden, in his *Essay of Dramatic
Poesy* (1668), admires Jonson for those virtues which com-
manded 'Augustan' respect: correctness, judgment, satirical

power and technical excellence. But he also gives force to the long comparison with Shakespeare which still reverberates in our own time, with Shakespeare as the original, Jonson the imitator. But if Jonson is neglected in our times, his methods and attitudes have influenced some of our modern dramatists – among them John Arden, Peter Barnes, David Turner and Charles Wood. Indeed, perhaps we should speak of Shakespeare as the great amateur and Jonson the great professional?

In spite of a certain obsolescence (realism means the portrayal of contemporary types who grow less and less relevant in contemporary language that grows out of date), his comedies held the stage for a long time. *Volpone* remained popular until about 1785, albeit in adapted forms. Then romanticism found it uncongenial. Jonson was neither a skylark nor a nightingale, merely a partridge. When a romantic critic admired Jonson it was because he could detect, as Swinburne* does in *Volpone*, 'a savour of something like romance'. Modern criticism was given impetus by the great edition of C. H. Herford, Percy and Evelyn Simpson in eleven volumes (1925–52), by T. S. Eliot's essay of 1919*, and by the work of such critics as L. C. Knights (1937)*, who related the twin evils of lust and greed in *Volpone* to the age in which he lived. But the fact remains that the version of the play that was popular from about 1921 on was the adaptation by Stefan Zweig which gives the play a happy ending.

Is *Volpone*, then, a comedy? Eliot offers the terms 'burlesque' or 'farce' while conceding that, in dealing with the unique world of Ben Jonson, neither term will 'appease the desire for definition'. But it is something more than the desire for definition: it is a question of how we feel when we leave the theatre at the end of the play. Enid Welsford in *The Fool* (1935), for example, suggests that 'when the mood of contempt is predominant – as for instance at the end of Jonson's *Volpone* – one feels that comedy is losing its character and turning into pure satire . . .'. When Jonson turned back to comedy after the failure of *Sejanus* it was to a kind of comedy different from his earlier work and hard to accommodate even within the elastic notions of comic art held by the Elizabethans. In the sternness of its catastrophe and the menacing quality of its main characters it came nearer Jonson's own view of tragedy (which,

again, was different from Shakespeare's profoundly moving,
human tragedies). His prologue speaks of 'quick comedy,
refined' and argues for the rightness of his ending. Whether or
not his arguments succeed with us, they certainly compel the
audience to *think* about the ending. Is it right? True? Just?

For many it is none of these things. Thus Coleridge* (*Literary
Remains*, 1836) found it difficult to maintain any pleasurable
interest in a tale where 'there is no goodness of heart in any of
the prominent characters', and felt that the play, after Act III,
became not a dead 'but a painful weight on the feelings'. His
solution was to diminish the role of Volpone and turn Celia into
the ward or niece of Corvino instead of his wife, and to make
Bonario her lover. Here Coleridge was almost certainly
remembering the version by Ludwig Tieck (whom he entertained at Highgate in 1817). Tieck's version, *Herr Von Fuchs*
(1793) did just that. Celia (renamed Louise) is the ward of
Corvino (Rabe) who is trying to match her with an old
pantaloon but is willing for her to marry Herr von Fuchs if that
will help get a legacy. Bonario (Karl) and Celia are already in
love and very much the hero and heroine of this version, and
when all evil schemes are exposed the judges restore to the ward
her property, giving her freedom from the faithless guardian.
As the curtain falls she tells the 'hero' that she is his forever.

When Yeats saw Jonson's version of the play in 1921 he felt
very much like Coleridge, remarking on the pathetic aspect of
Celia and Bonario who were not even lovers. But he went on to
grasp both the difficulty and the greatness of *Volpone* by
observing that 'this excites us because it makes us share in
Jonson's cold implacability'.

3   GOLD FEVER

Where tragedy was required to deal with far-away stately and
portentous matters in suitably stately language, comedy's
object was to deal with real life presenting, as Cicero expresses
it, 'a copy of life, a mirror of custom, a representation of truth'.
In his prologue to the revised version of *Every Man in his Humour*
Jonson rejected plays about larger matters like the Wars of the
Roses in favour of such deeds and language as men would

actually perform and use, and advocated presenting characters
such as comedy would choose

> When she would shew an image of the times
> And sport with human follies, not with crimes.

Watching *Volpone*, many have felt that 'follies' is not quite the
right word to describe what happens in the play and that the
characters are monsters rather than men.

Much of the darkness, the 'implacability', of the play comes
from its exotic setting: Venice. Jonson moved easily from the
Roman tragedy of Sejanus to the history of the Fox, and found
in the old Roman institution of legacy-hunting a better material
for comedy than, say, alchemy, though both in the Renaissance
atmosphere of speculation and adventuring were legitimate
alternatives in the general rush after wealth. This Roman
custom was, however, un-English which, from Jonson's point
of view, was a disadvantage. However, in the long run, it has
proved to be the play's strength. *Every Man in his Humour* was
removed from Florence to London and the characters renamed;
and in the prologue to *The Alchemist* (1610) Jonson explicitly
rejects Illyria in favour of London because his own city could
provide enough examples of manners, 'now called humours', to
keep a dramatist in business for a lifetime. Topical examples of
folly, local manners and custom soon 'date', so the general idea
of greed which fuels both *Volpone* and *The Alchemist* is less
restricted in *Volpone* to a particular time and place. Another loss
is imaginative, in the language, as a comparison between the
openings of the two plays makes clear. *The Alchemist* gives us rich,
realistic colloquial speech which often baffles us as much as the
language of alchemy, whereas *Volpone* has powerful verse. It is a
power we feel only occasionally in *The Alchemist* – for example in
the speeches of Sir Epicure Mammon.

Jonson's Jacobean audience, when not confronted with
contemporary London (as in his other comedies), needed at
least a modern society. So Jonson translates ancient Rome into
modern Italy, the classic setting for sensational evil-doing in
Jacobean drama. Whether Jonson's relationship with the
chaplain to the Venetian ambassador suggested this city to him
or not, Venice was exactly right as a location: a city based, as
Shakespeare also saw it, on trade and money-making. Jonson's

Venice, however, is not the vague city of Shakespeare's plays but a definite urban society, built up of intimate realistic detail culled from the writings of his friend John Florio; and it goes without saying that his English visitors are drawn from life as well as from a fourth-century Greek called Libanius. And Venice suggests Italy in general – with Rome (the seat of the Papacy) and Florence, whose son Machiavelli wrote about power as something imposed on others by superior intelligence rather than as delegated from God. So the man most likely to succeed is the man who is clever, bold, ruthless and adaptable.

Volpone's stratagem is based on truth: he is rich, a magnifico, without any family. He is not at all like the rogues in *The Alchemist* who follow their profession to avoid starvation. Nor is he in the grip of the fever of avarice that obsesses his clients. Indeed, some critics have argued that the opening speech is proof of how Volpone is *not* enmeshed in the blasphemy but is 'toying mischievously' with the perversion rather than deeply committed to it. Thus Alexander Leggat goes on to argue (in 'The Suicide of Volpone', *University of Toronto Quarterly*, 39, 1969) that Volpone's real perversion is that he regards life as a play where he can write the script for his own amusement: his sin is not to treat money as a god but to treat people as puppets. This is a perceptive comment. The chief of the deadly sins was Pride or Vanity, and it is this which motivates Volpone and (partly) Mosca. They are both politicians, Machiavels and truly representative of their time.

L. C. Knights* has reminded us of the relationship between literature and society, of the rise of capitalism in the Elizabethan and Jacobean period made possible by the large amounts of gold and silver which came from the New World. This helps to account for the rise of financiers (many with international status) and of the opportunities for spending. Such opportunities led to luxury and ostentation, to alchemy, the gulling of young heirs, fortune-hunting and usury. The doctrines of medieval society were incompatible with the demands of the capitalist, and so theory gave way to practice: individualism was the creed of the commercial classes.

To dramatise the dangers of greed and individualism (as he saw them), Jonson turned to a beast fable in the manner of Aesop: the story of the fox and the birds. A fox (*volpe* in Italian) who is growing too old to catch his prey pretends to be dying to attract birds that eat dead meat and, to complete the picture of death, a fly (*mosca*) hovers over his carcase. Reynard is a clever actor, resourceful, humorous but also greedy and sinister. One of the traditional associations of the fox was Machiavelli who recommended to his prince that he should adopt the animals reigning in his nature, suggesting that the most useful combination would be that of the fox and the lion. Jonson saw in this device exactly what he wanted and something that would test the intelligence of his audience, who would not be deceived by the clever acting into forgetting the more basic, sinister aspects of the fox. But, whereas in the beast fable we see animals who are like human beings, in *Volpone* we meet human beings who behave like animals. For a vulture or a raven or a crow to hover round the dead body of a fox may not be a pretty sight, but it is natural; scavengers cleanse the landscape. When we see a Venetian lawyer, an old gentleman and a wealthy merchant denying their human nature and reason, behaving like carrion-eaters, the spectacle is unnatural and chilling. Jonson carries the allegory over into the subplot where Sir Politick Would-be (Pol, the parrot) is finally turned into a tortoise having provoked Peregrine (the hawk). Jonson wisely used foreign names not simply for their appropriateness of the Venetian setting but because they make a stronger impression. If Volpone were called 'Reynard' and (say) Corvino 'Mr Crow', the effect would be comical, even satiric, but scarcely sinister.

This leads to a problem in staging *Volpone*. Jonson recalls the beast fable in his opening scenes; but how far should a director stress that fable by disguising his actors as birds and animals? E. B. Partridge* is surely correct when he says 'don't' to this. To present the characters in animal disguise would, once more, be comical or satiric but it would disturb the comparison Jonson is making: 'Probably Voltore was dressed to suggest a vulture . . . but he would always have been seen as a man' (Partridge, *The Broken Compass*, 1958).

The disease that has turned men into beasts is the lust for gold. They live in the gold-centred universe so effectively presented to us in the first scene, where gold replaces all moral, ethical and ideal values – and, indeed, every other appetite.

Volpone and Mosca are, initially, suggested as being unin-
volved in a world where food, drink and sex are either gold or as
gold. They claim to be more concerned with 'cunning purchase' than with possession, and Volpone uses his gold for
pleasure. Indeed Volpone claims that getting out of the charge
of attempted rape is better than actually enjoying Celia: 'The
pleasure of all woman-kind's not like it' [v ii 11]. So we watch
as he changes from magnifico to sick man to mountebank
doctor to virile lover to dying man to commendatore – and, at
last, to the fox himself. Some critics have objected to the
mountebank scene as over-long for what it contributes to the
play (a glimpse of Celia) and because it may have been
composed independently. But it shows us a great deal about
Volpone. For much of the play he is confined to bed where he is
offered services by Mosca much as a pimp offers his prostitute
for purchase. In St Mark's Square he shows us what he can
really do. He dazzles both audiences – the one on the stage and
the one in the auditorium – giving us irrefutable proof that he is
a great actor. But our response must not be simple: Celia is
sufficiently impressed to drop her handkerchief, but Peregrine
remains sceptical.

Mosca, too, is no ordinary servant. By dint of intelligence,
cunning and no mean acting ability, he has obtained the
position of parasite or personal asistant to a great man, and is
the agent for three wealthy Venetians. He can compose and
choreograph a masque, transform his master into an invalid,
arrange for the 'viewing' of Celia and later devise to get her into
his bedroom (if not his bed), and – most brilliantly of all –
organise the charade in court afterwards. He can get out of a
tricky situation, such as the one facing him when Voltore enters
unseen and overhears him talking to Corbaccio [iii ix]; he can
weep at will and hide from the world and Volpone his true
ambition: to wear the habit of a *clarissimo* (gentleman). But in
the end his true nature, greed, destroys him. He will not be
satisfied with merely half of Volpone's wealth and, like Sejanus
in Jonson's previous play, he miscalculates what his master is
capable of, and ends as a galley slave.

Both men, in short, enjoy the sport of improvisation, the
challenge of achieving the impossible, and both are actors who
take a professional interest in their performances.

The basic strands of the play, then, are gold, disease and transformation. Mosca's masque in Act I is a full statement of the theme and its implications. The limping verse gives us a clue to the burlesque of the Pythagorean theory of transmigration of souls. Here, says Nano, pointing to the hermaphrodite fool, is the only possible container at the present time for the soul of Pythagoras which first came from the god Apollo. Similarly the powder that Scoto offers the crowd in Act II came from Apollo, but the powder that made Venus a goddess is now a hair-rinse or mouth-wash! If men debase and degrade their noblest essence, the result will be monstrosity and folly. The degradation and folly of the clients we can immediately perceive and judge; but since role playing in the theatre is something to be applauded, and Volpone and Mosca do it very well, Jonson was faced with the problem of ending the play in such a way that he could punish vice but reward theatrical excellence.

John Dryden*, rather awkwardly, decided that the fifth act was excellent because in it Jonson gained the proper end of the play: the punishment of vice. But he had already detected the presence of two actions, the first ending naturally with Act IV, the second forced from Act V. He accommodated this second action by observing that, if Volpone's last disguise did not suit the character of a crafty or covetous person, it did suit Volpone's other trait of voluptuousness. John Dennis (1696)* is certainly more honest when he condemns the last Act where Volpone 'behaves himself like a Giddy Coxcombe, in the conduct of that very Affair which he manag'd so craftily in the first four . . .'. In his article 'The Suicide of Volpone' (mentioned above) Alexander Leggatt has argued, plausibly, that the impulse behind Act V is deeply rooted in Volpone's nature. If his sin is to treat life as a scenario (and other people as puppets to be manipulated) his instinct by the end of Act IV is to bring the play to an end. His ploy has been going on for three years and by pretending to die and leaving Mosca as the heir Volpone achieves the perfect comic climax – and Mosca agrees. What Volpone does not foresee is that he removes himself from the centre of the stage. Mosca undeceiving the clients is richly satisfying, but Volpone hiding behind a curtain to observe is less so, and he soon finds he has lost the initiative. In

unmasking he regains it and, moreover, displaces a rival artist
with brisk assurance:

> I am Volpone, and this is my knave;
> This, his own knave; this, avarice's fool;
> This, a chimera of wittol, fool, and knave;
> And, reverend fathers, since we all can hope
> Nought, but a sentence, let's not now despair it.
> You hear me brief.

Brief it may be, but it is splendid.

The actor playing the role can, if he wish, approach the role
in simpler terms and in the manner prescribed by Stanislavsky.
It will still amount to more or less the same thing as Leggatt's
argument. Volpone lacks any relationship – social or emotional; he is not a miser and he is easily bored. The device at the
beginning of the play has been running for three years and the
pleasure of gulling the clients is wearing thin (though the fact
that they have endured it all for three years emphasises the
obsessive nature of their greed). Mosca offers distractions – a
masque, and then Celia. He is even reduced to contriving that
Bonario shall overhear his father disinherit him to add spice to
the situation. Both these last two stratagems get tangled, but
Mosca is able to snatch triumph from the jaws of disaster.
Volpone's relief at being spared is brief. A glass or two of wine
and the humour is frighted from his heart [v i]; a few lines later
he is praising his 'exquisite' Mosca and rejoicing in the pleasure
he got out of escaping from the rape charge (and seeing all his
clients make fools of themselves and the Court). Then he must
be doing something once more. Jonson makes the two plays in
the last act below the standard of those in previous acts, and not
merely because Volpone is onlooker rather than participant.
All Mosca's plays give the fools flattering images of themselves,
persuading them that they are noble and will be rich. All this
produces handsome results: gold, plate and jewels which find
their way into Mosca's hands and Volpone's treasury. Mosca's
plays leave illusions intact and strong, but Volpone's plays
show the legacy-hunters as greedy fools and dupes, and they
strike back. Mosca is also revealed as an opportunist, which
should not be news to us.

Gold fever is present in the Court scenes too. The justice

meted out here is familiar; this court accepts bribes, is readily swayed by the rhetoric of a lawyer and, later, proposes a daughter as wife to the parasite whom gold has turned into a noble man. When they perceive the truth (by a miracle according to the First Avocatore!), the judges mete out punishments with a severity possibly strengthened by the knowledge that they have been made fools of. The sentences at least square the appearances of the characters with their reality. Celia's plea for mercy goes unheard and she and Bonario stand on the side-lines, commenting piously on Heaven's grace. Their words may remind us of higher values but they also underline the fact that this 'happy' ending has been produced neither by justice nor grace. The law cannot be guaranteed to deal fairly with people, but it might. Jonson remains true to the negatives of the play.

Volpone is not a realistic play because it shows us a special world (these flat characters could not step out into any other world), and the forces which might ordinarily halt the obsessions are ignored or expelled so that we can see the unrestricted effects of delusion and folly. We cannot pity such characters since they have made their own god and chained themselves to it; but they make us feel the value of freedom and of reason; of humanity. In *Volpone* everyone is either a knave or a fool. The knaves have wit, intelligence and act well, but in the end neither condition is desirable. Jonson insists that crime does not pay, not because of the law or of religion, but because success for a criminal leads to that state where the criminal cannot keep within any limits at all. The only detached character in the play is Peregrine, who is powerless to stem the tide of folly and never in the main plot. He can remove Sir Pol but no more, and even this slight improvement throws up in reverse, and ironically, the concerns of the main plot where no improvement is possible: no cure exists for Volpone and his world. The idea that Zweig's version of the play is superior because it liberates the gold must be rejected. It is true that Zweig is embracing, rather vaguely, a Marxist view that gold should be distributed, but for Jonson gold is not a neutral thing which is evil only in the wrong hands; for Jonson gold is itself a positive danger.

4   THE DOUBLE PLOT

It was accepted practice in the Elizabethan theatre for a
playwright to take his plot or story from another work and
elaborate on this basic structure. So, for most of the plays of
Shakespeare we can point to a particular source. But in *Volpone*
(as mentioned in section 1, Introduction, above), though it
draws on many elements from its author's wide learning, the
action is Jonson's own. T. S. Eliot* insists that Jonson's
dramatic skill lies not so much in writing a good plot as in doing
without a plot. What plot there is in *Volpone* is just enough to
keep the players in motion, and should rather be called an
'action' than a 'plot'.

Possibly Eliot was over-reacting to the continual praise for
Jonson's craftsmanship (if your characters are humours who do
not develop, then any development achieved *must* be through
the plot); but, in fact, critics have always expressed doubts
about the plot of *Volpone*. Dryden* found 'the unity of design . . .
not exactly observed in it', and was disturbed that the first
action terminated at the end of Act IV while a second action was
forced from it in Act V. By comparison with *Epicœne, or The Silent
Woman* (1609), where the business rises in every act, each scene
bringing forth new difficulties until 'the audience is brought
into despair that the business can naturally be effected', *Volpone*
is deficient. John Dennis*, as we have seen, found the
behaviour of Volpone in Act V inconsistent and describes the
Politick Would-be pair as 'Excrescencies' which have nothing
to do with the design of the play. Hazlitt*, conceding that
Volpone was Jonson's best play – 'prolix and improbable, but
intense and powerful' – still found the whole 'worked up
mechanically, and our credulity overstretched at last revolts
into scepticism, and our attention flags into drowsiness'.

Jonson himself, in *Timber*, insisted that the action in either
tragedy or comedy should be 'let grow till the necessity asks a
Conclusion', and for this only two things need be considered:
that the action take place in one day, and that 'there be place
left for digression, and Art'. So even if the subplot were proved
to be a digression, it would not go against his principles. In fact
the subplot is not a digression and the main plot is tight, logical
and without redundancy.

The whole play revolves round the bed or the court of law, and the function of both has been perverted. The action occupies one day, opening at sunrise, moving through the morning with the mountebank scene. In the afternoon Volpone receives Lady Would-be and Celia. The fourth Act takes place in the late afternoon, and the Court promises to pass sentence on Celia and Bonario before the end of the day. Although the Duchess of Newcastle* (in the third preface of her *Playes*, 1662) may have a point in suggesting that no rational person could believe that so much could happen in the course of one day, Jonson uses the unity of time (as Shakespeare uses it in two of his plays) to put pressure on the characters. The zest with which Volpone and Mosca attack every minute of the day increases our sense of excitement (and our awareness of the blankness and boredom of Volpone's life should he relax the pace for a minute), and the short space of time emphasises the suddenness with which one's luck can change.

Volpone at the centre of the play and its world offers his gold as a lure for greedy acquaintances. The gold is genuine, his sickness is not. But because he must feign sickness he must remain in bed, and the management of the action, therefore, lies in the hands of his parasite. Act I presents three clients visiting him: Voltore, a lawyer; Corbaccio, who although old and deaf 'yet hopes to hop / Over his grave' and who is persuaded to disinherit his son making Volpone his heir; and Corvino, a young merchant. All three are driven by the same folly but each is given different circumstances for dramatic variety and to suggest the extent of the disease. Corbaccio is deaf and old, and so can discuss medical symptoms (and cures) from his own experience; but when Corvino arrives Volpone is blind and deaf, so Mosca and the new visitor have the pleasure of shouting insults at him. It is before the arrival of Corvino that Mosca has to apply a little more eye make-up. Corvino has no objection to Mosca smothering Volpone so long as he is not present! After they have gone Volpone and Mosca talk about the fourth client, Lady Politick Would-be (wife of an English visitor to Venice), and a discussion on wives leads naturally to Corvino's wife, Celia – 'Bright as your gold! and lovely as your gold!' – introduced as a diversion rather than a complication.

The challenge of getting through Corvino's defences and

seeing Celia cheers Volpone up. It liberates him (literally) and, disguised as Scoto of Mantua, he entertains the crowd and draws Celia to her window [Act II]. In that crowd are Peregrine (another English traveller) and Sir Politick who, for once, is correct in detecting a plot in this apparently harmless entertainment. The jealous Corvino arrives to drive the crowd away and beat Volpone who is wounded (by the sight of Celia and the blows of her husband), but none the less for that interested in how well he performed his role as mountebank. 'The Turk is not more sensual in his pleasure / Than will Volpone', he has said in Act I, but then he goes on to catalogue his pearl, diamant and chequeens. The actor playing Volpone has to decide just how sensual Volpone is. In the scene with Celia, for example, does the boasting conceal inadequacy? Are we to take the endless disguises with which copulation is dressed up as a sign that he can only perform in exotic circumstances and with a lot of props? Here, too, the actor playing Mosca might take a hint of his plot against Volpone from the line 'and, yet, I would / Escape your *epilogue*' [II iv 34]. Corvino berates Celia, threatening her with the famous chastity belt until Mosca arrives to announce that Volpone is much improved (with the help of Scoto's famous elixir) and now needs a young woman to complete the cure. Signior Lupo (Mr Wolf) has already offered his daughter. Corvino tells Celia to dress for a visit to old Volpone where she will indeed learn how free her husband is from jealousy or fear over her honour.

Mosca has reason to be pleased with himself, and Act III, scene i shows him very pleased with his own cleverness which he soon illustrates by charming a contemptuous Bonario, Corbaccio's son, into belief in his goodness. Meanwhile Volpone, who has feigned sickness to lure his clients to his house, has attracted Lady Would-be, and he who traps by words is now trapped in her relentless chatter until Mosca arrives and improvises on her sexual jealousy, sending her away with a tale of amours in gondolas engaged in by her spouse, Sir Politick. Bonario is introduced into the house [Act IV], but the merchant-client Corvino arrives too soon with Celia, so Bonario has to be left in the gallery while Volpone courts Celia, eventually threatening violence to get his will of her. She is rescued from rape by Bonario, and for the plotters all seems lost. The knocking on the door, however, is not the police but Corbaccio (and later Voltore, unobserved), both of whom Mosca is able to beguile in turn, so that when the action moves to the courtroom, Celia and Bonario are confronted by the three clients, and also by Lady Would-be (her ladyship believing Mosca's tale that Celia is her husband's paramour). A 'dying' Volpone is carried in and acquitted by the judges.

This leaves Jonson with a fifth and final act in which to disentangle the truth. There seems no possibility of this happening since Volpone's situation is impregnable. But the Fox, exultant at the triumph of his 'exquisite' Mosca, and perhaps a little drunk, decides to play another game. Sending forth his dwarf and eunuch to advertise his death, he waits behind the curtain while Mosca, splendidly dressed as his heir, takes an inventory and dismisses the clients one by one. Even this is not enough for Volpone, who wants to mock them in a reassembled courtroom, and so takes on the disguise of a commendatore. But just as, in a subsidiary development, a disguised Peregrine (earlier thought by Lady Would-be to be the woman in her husband's case) has forced Sir Pol into a tortoise shell, so now a disguised Mosca has Volpone in a disguise from which there is no escape. In Act v scene v, Mosca is satisfied with half of his master's wealth; but now the desire to achieve the genteel status of *clarissimo* is all-powerful, and eventually [v xii] half proves not enough. Volpone realises his disastrous mistake when he meets his dwarf and fool running through the streets. But he will not let himself be cheated by a common parasite. He reveals himself, accepting the sentence of the Court with dry relish.

The subplot is obviously tied into the main plot by Lady Would-be, who becomes the client Volpone could do without. Another connection is that Sir Politick Would-be believes himself to be a politician like Volpone and Mosca (and, indeed invites Peregrine to be his front man in Act iv). When Lady Would-be moves from the main plot to attack Peregrine, whom she takes to be a courtesan dressed as a boy, the young Englishman takes his revenge by hunting Sir Politick into the tortoise case. It tells us something about Sir Politick that he has the shell to hand (just as we guess something about Corvino because he keeps a chastity belt in the house).

But even the most recent reviewers seem to regard all this as tedious and any director must be tempted to cut out the subplot altogether, to save time and to concentrate the audience's mind on the main action. But, however loose the connections are, they are very strong. Jonson claims in his prologue that the play's author has produced a comedy 'as best critics have designed', observing the laws of time, place and persons, but then adds the disclaimer: 'From no needful rule he swerveth.' The important word is 'needful'. Aristotle should be honoured but he is not a dictator, and Jonson reserves the right to do what he thinks best. Yet for over two hundred years critics have dismissed the subplot as something that 'never did, nor ever can please' (Peter Whalley*, 1756), and even sympathetic critics have only been able to offer the subplot as a comic relief in the main plot (with Lady Would-be) and from the main plot (with Sir Politick). It provides relaxation, and the relatively harmless folly of the Would-be couple makes the crimes in the main action seem even darker: English silliness contrasted with Italian vice. More recently scholars, and in particular Jonas A. Barish* ('The Double Plot in Volpone', 1953), have argued for a closer thematic relationship between the two plots and suggested that neither Jonson's imagination nor his ear for detail have faltered here.

The Politick Would-be pair are indeed alien to the ways of Venice and difficult to fit in, though one still meets them there (nowadays they are often American). They have their place in the beast fable as parrots, just as Peregrine their fellow-countryman is both a traveller and a hawk. The loquaciousness of parrots is immediately obvious – and not just in Lady Would-be – and we should remember that parrots imitate the speech of others rather than speaking words of their own thinking. This English couple, therefore, should be seen as mimics (and should not some credit be given for their immensely comic performance as such?). It is Lady Would-be's 'humour' to visit Venice to learn the language and so forth. Both husband and wife seek to imitate the behaviour of the Venetians and, without knowing it, parody in their Englishness the action of the main plot. Sir Politick's prodigies in England – lions whelping in the Tower, fires at Berwick or a whale discovered in the river as far up as Woolwich – and his talk about Stone, the fool, now dead, as a secret agent who received messages in cabbages, are certainly more comic than the monsters we meet in Venice. But they warn us that English follies could, if we are not careful, turn into Italian vices. Sir Politick, as his full name implies, would be a Machiavelli, revelling in plots and deceptions and uncovering intrigues; while his wife apes the manners of local women, reads Italian poets and aspires to rival the Venetians in the art of seduction. Sir Politick is unsuccessful, whereas Volpone continues to amass profit and pleasure from his schemes. Yet perhaps it would be more accurate to say that this couple are out of their depth rather than out of place: amateurs in a world of professionals.

In the main action Lady Would-be contrasts her antics with the more sinister gestures of her rival legacy-hunters, amongst which murder is suggested. She is jealous, like Corvino; foolishly erudite, like Voltore; and she gets herself into a compromising situation with Mosca, like Corbaccio. She also serves as a contrast with Celia. The discussion of wives in Act I moves from Lady Would-be to Celia, while in Act III the visit of Lady Would-be to Volpone's bedchamber precedes that of Celia. Volpone ruefully reflects [III iv 78] that the 'highest female grace is silence'. The English lady's fondness for cosmetics, her endless chatter, her lecherous nature and her would-be seduction of Volpone, all set the stage for Volpone's attempt on Celia's virtue. Celia hardly speaks at all, scorns cosmetics and finds herself lost in the changing shapes of the play. These changing shapes, announced in the masque in Act I, continue until the end of the play: only Bonario and Celia do not ape others or change their shape in the whole play. Even Peregrine assumes a disguise to gull Sir Politick.

But since her ladyship only 'would be', and can be convicted of folly not crimes, such folly as hers needs no external authority to punish it. She resolves to quit Venice and take to the sea 'for physick' at about the same time that Peregrine and the merchants transform Sir Politick into a tortoise. Aspiring to be everything he is not, Sir Politick demonstrates the ridiculousness of his behaviour by crawling under the shell of another animal to save himself. He hides under this shell as Volpone hides in his sick-bed, and he is unshelled as Volpone is uncased in the last Act. Curious about prodigies, Sir Politick has become one himself: half human, half animal. His punishment is complete. So both the would-be couple, characters which surely survive from the early humour comedies, can now be seen as out of their humour, cured by ridicule. Having dealt with the imitations of vice, Jonson is at liberty to turn to the real thing.

If the tortoise scene fits the pattern of the play it may be an example of Jonson sacrificing, for once, dramatic art to scholarship. Nicholas Boileau* (in the Soames/Dryden translation-adaptation, *The Art of Poesy*, 1683) lamented:

> When in the *Fox* I see the tortoise hist,
> I lose the author of the *Alchemist*.

Many subsequent critics have agreed. The eighteenth century dismissed it as too farcical, and its defenders have mainly argued that it passes time while Mosca gets the commendatore drunk to acquire his uniform for Volpone. Yet it is interesting that in Act IV scene i Sir Politick, still fretting about the mountebank scene (which he rightly observes was a plot) and pretending to be a man of projects who needs an assistant, introduces the character of the commendatore in preparation for Act V. Donald Wolfit cut the scene completely. His 1942 prompt book reads: '2 mins. wait for Mr Wolfit's change', while in his 1944 production he interpolated a sequence between Mosca and the real commendatore, drunk and suitless.

But for the contemporary reader and some of the contemporary audience (particularly those at the universities), the tortoise as an emblem of policy and silence was an appropriate end for Sir Politick, while its presence under the foot of Venus in art reminded those in the know that it symbolised the two qualities of a chaste woman: she is silent, and she always keeps to her own house. Thus the shell continues to suggest the contrast between Lady Would-be and Celia. The scene fails in our time, not because of its farcical nature, but because Jonson may not have subdued erudition to dramatic ends. A knowledge of Catullus and Ovid deepens our response to the scene where Volpone woos Celia, but ignorance about them does not blunt the dramatic effect of that scene or their part in it. Here allusions that have lost their force are needed for the scene to work on every level; some would say on any level.

5 PARASITES OR SUB-PARASITES

Mosca sees the whole world as little else but 'parasites or sub-parasites'. He defines the true parasite (and he counts himself in this superior breed) as one born with the art of being.

> Present to any humour, all occasion;
> And change a visor, swifter than a thought.

The rest of the world is made up of zanies or fools to be handled by such an artist. This is a fitting description of the world of the play but it is a harsh view of society, of man's need for others and his interdependence expressed in terms of love, marriage, family, friendship or loyalty to a creed or country or even integrity in business. Jonson makes his point about society by the firmness with which such beneficial aspects of social behaviour are excluded from the play. His characters are members of a circus and Volpone is ringmaster, for Volpone needs an audience to work with and on; he cannot bear to be left on his own for very long.

In creating these characters Jonson has long been saddled with the label 'humours'. It was his own fault since he practically took out a patent on the term. But where he ridiculed the follies of the time in *Every Man in his Humour*, by *Every Man out of his Humour* the term had deepened to mean something more than a simple affectation. It had become something deep seated in a character, a ruling passion:

> As when some one peculiar quality
> Doth so possess a man that it doth draw
> All his affect, his spirits, and his powers,
> In their confluxions, all to run one way,
> This may be truly said to be a humour.

The description of such humours was, John Dryden insisted, the peculiar genius and talent of Ben Jonson. Thus the comparison grew that where Shakespeare's characters are human beings who could stray out of the world of the play into

our streets, those of Jonson were flat, incapable of existing
outside the play; more, as Hazlitt put it, 'like machines,
governed by mere routine, or by the convenience of the poet
whose property they are'. The danger of this, as Hazlitt
remarked when reviewing *Every Man in his Humour* in 1816, is
that manners and humours tend to become obsolete, and 'being
in themselves altogether arbitrary and fantastical, have
become unintelligible and uninteresting'.

   T. S. Eliot* was wise, I think, to dismiss the definition of
Jonson as a writer of comedy of humours. He probably felt that,
if he could get rid of this and the cliché about plot, he might get
people to read Jonson with a fresh and open mind. The
description properly fits only two early comedies and can
hardly be applied even to the characters in the subplot of
Volpone. Even so, the play's characters are conceived on the
'humours' plan where a master passion dominates speech and
behaviour, and such singleness of purpose concentrates the
energy of a character and propels him forward with undeviat-
ing certainty. *Volpone* is remarkable because it presents us not
with a variety of humours but with a single humour, and the
minor characters need be no more than theatrical types,
puppets, because they are worked by Mosca and Volpone and
exhibit nothing else but their humour. Such characters do not
grow, and so at the end of the play there can be no question of
anybody living happily ever after because they really have no
life to begin with: most of the characters were revealed as full
entities at their very first entrance. (By *Bartholomew Fair* (1614),
Jonson is changing his method so that the comedy, long as it is,
has the air of being the prologue to a changed life afterwards!)
Again we must except Volpone. He is a character who is
capable of surprising us – as Shakespeare's characters do –
particularly in the last Act. He has not completely lost his life in
his vice and, caring for the game more than the profit, refuses at
the end to be blackmailed by a common dependant: or, in
theatrical terms, to be up-staged by another actor.

   Moreover, Hazlitt, in his review of *Every Man in his Humour*
makes an observation that is always true of Jonson. He admits
that the play acts better than it reads and notes that the power
of the stage can give reality and interest to what would
otherwise be without either. If each of the minor characters is

stripped down to a single passion (and all, in fact, to the same passion), the *persona* is nevertheless rich in human detail. Thus Corbaccio, the raven – a bird with a loud, harsh and croaking voice – is deaf. Should he, then, be played with that loud toneless voice characteristic of a deaf man? Jonson wanted realism and so could hardly avoid this human trait. Moreover each character was to recall the human being *before* disease and deformity overtook him. The law of persons also required Jonson to present a character who was typical, so that the interaction of characters would be typical of human society. The resultant action would be an imitation of life that would be universally true with a moral that was universally applicable. And, of course, an actor cannot act in a two-dimensional way; he is provided here with a text that gives him the roundness of characterisation suitable for the new picture frame-stage which was taking over from the old Elizabethan acting area.

Volpone throws himself into his roles with all the energy of a disciple of Stanislavsky. Appearing first as the great Venetian lord, he is transformed before our very eyes into a sick old man who then appears as the flamboyant quack doctor (disease is profitable from either point of view), then as a lover, a dying man, a commendatore and, at last, the fox himself. Or rather, not quite 'at last', for his final shape appears when delivering the epilogue: here he is the actor who has presented us with the Fox in all his shapes and now claims his reward (or punishment). Blue Proteus is Volpone's rival [III vii 153] but his principle weapon is not clothes or make-up but his rhetoric, and our attitude to him must be qualified by his use of words. We should at least be ambivalent towards him. Even in the splendid opening speeches the interjections of Mosca ought to warn us that this actor, his master, is made up of vanity and pride. But he is a professional. When he plays the mountebank he captures the spiel of a huckster; and, in spite of Peregrine's scorn, Scoto of Mantua is a very superior mountebank. (Jonson, incidentally, got the name from an Italian juggler who visited the court of Elizabeth in 1576.)

If Volpone's easy acceptance of Mosca's flattery does not alert us, then the sight of his household should. Mosca's claim that the dwarf, eunuch and hermaphrodite-fool are Volpone's children, along with other bastards begot on beggars, gipsies,

Jews and blackamoors, may be a tale to frighten Corvino into giving more jewels, but they are physical examples of the folly and monstrosity which abounds in the play. It is possible to cite historical precedents for such collections – the Spanish Court of the period had a fine collection of dwarfs for its amusement – and their presence on the stage is both literal and symbolic. Moreover, in their masque they reduce classical learning and civilised values to a final stage of degeneracy and, on a functional level, run through the play to bring it to a close by warning Volpone of what he has done. For he has handed everything over to Mosca to vex the people who have so stupidly united to save him.

Mosca seizes the opportunity. Throughout the play he has been an extraordinary parasite, capable, intelligent and witty, but only the blind and the deaf would be taken in by his act. His proclaimed self-love [III i] should not surprise us, but neither should it suggest that he has been playing a deep game all along, introducing Celia to bring about the downfall of his master. He is gradually infected by his master's enthusiasm for game and profit. Bonario, too, lodged close to Volpone's bedchamber, must be seen as an accident and Mosca demonstrates his finest invention and wit in saving Volpone from that disaster. It is only when Volpone spontaneously offers him the keys to the treasury and dresses him up as a gentleman that he sees and seizes his chance. Mosca is not strictly a planner; rather he is an improviser, and even when he recognises the strength of his position he is at first prepared to let Volpone back into his hole for a price. But being deferred to is pleasant, and Mosca's idea of what his price will be rises as time passes until he is likely to be married to the daughter of the Fourth Avocatore and Volpone will be whipped. Mosca has underestimated the nature of his master, not recognising that pride and vanity can be stubborn values. It was this ending that Terry Hands found so overwhelming (*Gambit*, 6, no. 22, Jan. 1973):

There's a man who's reduced himself to the point of animal life, and then comes up with a piece of heroism which is always reserved for villains: like Macbeth tying himself to the stake. In Paris I saw a dreadful watered-down version by Stefan Zweig and Jules Romains which is widely popular; very consistent and French, all the subplots are out, and that moment of defiance is gone; it's just

Mosca's victory. But that moment is where the man comes out. [Volpone] says, 'It's mine; I'm going to take it with me.'

It is in the first court scene, too, in Act IV, that we see the minor characters' ability to change endlessly, assuming a common face of virtue against Bonario and Celia.

These two virtuous characters are helpless precisely because they cannot change or adapt to circumstances, and they have a touching (and foolish?) faith in truth and justice. As such they are inactive and tend to be a little dull. In the old morality plays the vices were shown as dangerously attractive but revealed at the end as foolish because it was foolish to fight against God. Spiritual goodness is not clever, it cannot disguise itself and it does not make jokes. We must still admire Volpone at the end because his wit is unquenched. (Even as he is led off to the hospital of the Incurabili he puns on the word 'mortify', which means humiliation, spiritual discipline *and* hanging game to make it tender!) Bonario and Celia have little to say. She asks for patience at the beginning of the play and mercy for her persecutors at the end, but neither appeal is heard; and, in Bonario's case, we must sympathise with any young actor, required to dash onto the stage with a drawn sword to rescue the heroine, who has to speak the lines Jonson gives him after the soaring splendours of Volpone's arias. Yet can we ignore what they stand for? As characters, certainly, Jonson renders them quite null and may be criticising through them that type of virtue which stands around and does nothing, relying on Heaven instead of fighting the good fight. To talk of their 'white innocence' may be to miss the point altogether. Nevertheless, the shadowy nature of these two characters is crucial to the design of the play. If they were to steal our sympathy then *Volpone* would be a play that simply condemns evil, and Jonson wishes it to be attractive. Even so, he cannot resist a complication with Celia who, in throwing down her handkerchief [II ii], presents us with a kind of problem; while Bonario is, after all, fighting for his inheritance (i.e. wealth) like anyone else.

Since in this play we can identify either with fools or with clever rogues, our identification with Volpone and Mosca is fairly automatic. This is the trap Jonson sets for us. The clients in Act I are Volpone's audience and they accept his perfor-

mance too readily and uncritically – Corbaccio's deafness is
symbolic of this. But we, the other audience, are, from the
beginning, challenged to do better. As we watch Voltore the
lawyer get to work in the first Court scene [IV v] – his tongue is
indeed tipped with gold – shifting the bench, which is originally
on the side of Celia and Bonario, until it acquits Volpone and
withdraws to consider suitable punishments for two such
reprobates, we are appalled at what language can do and how a
man can debase his profession by doing it so well. But we are
detached. We despise Voltore. When we listen to Volpone we
should not fall under his spell. But we do. It is probably not
until the scene with Celia, if then, that we part company with
him. Jonson's faith in classical and Christian values may not be
shared by today's audiences, and possibly was not shared
wholeheartedly by his contemporary audience, but by making
us laugh even as we come to terms with the horror that causes
the laughter, Jonson involves us in criminal proceedings. We
cannot judge the judges too harshly since we have fallen into
the same error. This involvement is too profound a relationship
to be solved by letting Bonario and Celia go off hand in hand
into the sunset at the end of the play. Volpone, in his epilogue,
steps forward to remind us that in the theatre we tend to acquit
criminals who have entertained us. Good theatre is that which
has pleased us in performance, and we can perceive why the
Church Fathers took a hesistant (and finally a critical) view
about the place of the theatre in Christian society. However,
since Jonson punishes the vicious amusingly, *Volpone* must, in
every sense, be seen as *good* theatre.

6   A LITTLE WIT

'The immediate appeal of Jonson', T. S. Eliot tells us, 'is to the
mind; his emotional tone is not in the single verse, but in the
design of the whole.' When critics reject headings such as
'theme', 'plot', 'humours' or 'satire' in favour of some larger
unity of inspiration, they reflect a critical difficulty in writing
about Jonson and *Volpone*. Such headings are at best a critical
convenience, but with Jonson they strike one as even more
redundant, since any discussion of theme, plot or character

slides into a discussion of language. Whatever happens on the stage, the beginning of performance is a text, the words on the page – and Jonson was very careful about them. He chose to print his plays so that the educated minority could savour all his allusions and ponder on his declared intention of reforming, single-handedly, stage poetry which, he believed, had sunk low in quality and esteem. The density of his text must, however, function in the theatre where the average audience, even at a play by Shakespeare, gets less than the text offers; and, indeed, the best actors under the best director can only offer less than what the text offers. Of course, Jacobean audiences were more used to listening in the theatre, and listening to verse drama, than we are. The present generation reads and watches television or films. Jonson already had some competition from the scenery of Inigo Jones but he fought passionately for the primacy of the spoken word.

Nevertheless, in considering the language of the play we cannot overlook the plot and particularly the catastrophe. In admiring Volpone and Mosca in the world of the play, our sympathy is involved and tested in the world outside the play. Volpone and his creed constituted only one challenge to the moral and social system built up over two thousand years by pagan and Christian thinkers, but it was a strong challenge. A Jacobean audience might well have a sneaking sympathy for Volpone and be as tempted by his aspirations and energetic pursuit of wealth, power and pleasure as any modern audience. It is the temptation the play still offers that gives it its timeless quality. Clearly Volpone and Mosca are not sympathetic characters in any ordinary sense, but up to a point we participate with glee in their stratagems and rejoice in their success. We are momentarily infected so that the object of satire is not external but actually in ourselves. But the infection should be temporary, and by Act v we should be completely detached (here, possibly, Celia, without doing very much, helps). We know that great satire seems to delight in what it attacks; only through such an ambivalent attitude can an author give his satire energy and delight and push us forward to that shocking moment when we recognise what it is we are celebrating. As Gerald Clarke put it in *Time* (October, 1977) Volpone is not only evil but 'endlessly beguiling'. If Volpone and Mosca are used, as L. C. Knights and D. J. Enright have claimed, to 'place' the other characters, they themselves are 'placed' by the exaggeration of their own language. In Jonson the master-wit is the one who outwits, and Volpone's language is assumed like his costumes and his make-up – and all three would be obvious to anyone not blinded by pride, avarice or ambition: anyone unwilling to suspend disbelief.

In the Jacobean theatre words were still the prime way an audience could know about character, and in Jonson there is a great deal to listen to. E. B. Partridge, analysing (in *The Broken Compass*) the opening of the play, finds four kinds of imagery working in the verse: religious, classical, animal and love. Jonson uses these images, he suggests, to present values implicit in the culture of his time and, by contrast, to recall a past but still powerful ideal. Thus religious imagery reminds us of what Volpone and his associates are betraying, just as the love imagery recalls great love affairs and confirms the absence of either greatness or love in this portrait of Venice. It is an economic way of telling us how foolish or vicious or comic the world of the play really is, and the method is nowhere better illustrated than in the opening scene of the play or, at its savage centre, the wooing of Celia. We examine these two episodes in the following section.

7 TWO EPISODES

The Opening: Act I, scene i
Alexander Leggatt (in 'The Suicide of Volpone') suggests that in the opening speech 'it is at least possible that Volpone is toying mischievously with this perversion, rather than deeply committed to it'. Thus, though there is a serious perversion of values, the imagery with which Volpone begins the day – and Leggatt points to the 'carefulness' with which he perverts religious language – is another entertainment which is left behind as he goes on to other amusements: the 'cheerful impudence of his language indicates that he enjoys the blasphemy for its own sake'. Jonson's problem is exposition. He wishes to throw us into the action of the play and as swiftly, and tellingly, as possible introduce us to themes, character, plot and

the point of view he thinks we should take. Volpone and Mosca tell one another things they already know, but what this opening scene is about is the *way* Jonson makes them tell these things to themselves (and us). With this proviso, then, let us consider its effect.

Although Jonson works primarily on our imagination through words, the *visual* effect of this opening scene should be stunning. The first rays of sun strike the glitter of Volpone's uncovered hoard. This is also our first view of the 'hero', the Fox, before he assumes his disguises. So the actor playing the role must decide what kind of Volpone he is. How old is he? What does he look like, and sound like?

Volpone should chant his hymn to gold, calling forth from the audience both admiration and shock. We should be charmed by the blasphemy of a world where gold replaces the sun as the centre and source of life, and where a gold coin replaces the wafer in the Sacrifice of the Mass (as in Tyrone Guthrie's 1968 production, where Volpone elevated the coin and proferred it, wafer-like, to a kneeling Mosca [I i 66–7]). A director will have to consider how shocking this stage image will be to a largely secular-minded audience.

Volpone describes here a new universe with new laws. He redefines history by invoking the Golden Age (that happy natural state according to the ancient poets) and substituting money for the bonds of blood, piety, love and friendship which in the past had held men together. Gold, too, confers upon men quickly what in the past they had had to labour long to achieve: virtue, fame, honour and all things else. This brave new world replaces our usual relationships with contracts based solely on gold: a master/servant relationship whose aim is to cheat the world and one another, if they can, of the only thing that is important. If Volpone has children they are bastards begotten for pleasure (and in drunkenness) and kept for pleasure. He has no parent, wife, child or friend, and so any 'friends' who visit him in his sickness are as counterfeit as the sickness, willing to hasten his end and their gain by poison or suffocation if need be. This speech, too, gives us the plot of the play. A son will be disinherited, a wife prostituted, Voltore will dishonour his profession, and the beauty of Celia can only be felt in terms of gold and silver. Ultimately we see how total the infection is,

since judges change their view of a man according to whether
he is rich or poor, and Volpone can only prevent Mosca from
getting married by shedding his last disguise.

Jonson presents us here with his view of the materialistic
culture of Jacobean England and its celebration of the individual; and, simultaneously, through the images and
metaphors, he reminds us of past values and ideals now
distorted and diseased. According to Volpone this is literally
the Golden Age, the best age, in which values and ideals qualify
gold rather than that gold is a suitable epithet for the ideals.
Volpone's imagination works on golden connections. It is
obviously the religion of the world: a saint in its shrine, the
world's soul and Volpone's, each piece a relic, a sacred treasure
in a blessed room. Its price is the price of souls, so that Hell with
it is worth more than heaven. The effect may be dulled
nowadays when our attitude often seems nearer Volpone's
than Jonson's. But, like the Jacobeans, we probably still pay
lip-service to the conventional Christian view – and by the
standards of that view these opening lines are blasphemous.

Gold as the centre of the universe is brighter than the sun,
and this reference moves Volpone's imagination to alchemy
where the sun is the father of gold (and the moon, which
receives the seeds of the sun, its mother). The sun also leads
him to astrology and the celestial Ram, the constellation that
heralds spring when the earth begins to stir and long for
sunshine, and, also, sexual activity. Gold is the source of all
creation, and hence literature has used the word to describe the
finest of things and times. Gold transcends (the religious
imagery is relentless) all joy in 'children, parents, friends', who
are as dreams on earth: real only as shadows of gold. Love, too,
is golden (following Homer, the Latin poets often called Venus
'golden'); and as silence is golden so the dear saint, the god, is
dumb. This paradox moves Volpone and, indeed, the whole
play: gold makes men speak and act, becoming almost a parody
of Aristotle's Unmoved Mover.

Unlike Marlowe in *Doctor Faustus*, Jonson does not introduce
his world and its morality with a soliloquy. Mosca breaks in,
the acolyte responding to the priest, in a dialogue that has the
air of daily ritual about it (as the Mass is celebrated every day).
No Christian humility here, however, but all the worldliness

and arrogance of a Venetian magnifico. And that arrogance is confirmed when Volpone claims that he gets his wealth in no common way. His clients want the wealth, but he delights in the way he gets it. His catalogue of 'common' ways of acquiring wealth is fascinating. He will not touch trade, agriculture, industry or money-lending for profit. The inclusion of 'men' in what mills grind is a splendid touch, and glass blowing and shipping remind us that this is Venice. Usury, too, recalls Shakespeare's savage play about Venice. Shylock hated Antonio most because of his opposition to usury. There had been general agreement that lending for gain by compact was evil, but this medieval view had had to yield to contemporary practice. The evils of usury were widely known, and many great Elizabethans (including the Queen) were in debt. But Bacon, in his essay 'Of Usury' (1625) had argued that it was inevitable, and Calvin and some modern theologians had reluctantly agreed that it had to be tolerated. Many Jacobeans would tacitly have agreed with Shylock's argument that money can be made to breed as well as sheep [*M. of V.*, i iii 65ff.]. Volpone's description of the ways of gaining wealth is a grim view of capitalist enterprise but not without its truth: we feed beasts for the slaughter-house, wound the earth with ploughs, mills exploit men, ships sink, and interest rates can cripple borrowers. The speech is also an audacious travesty of that golden age Volpone recalled in his opening speech. Ovid describes this age as a time when the pine tree had not been felled to take men to other lands and the earth, untouched by plough or hoe, gave forth food for men to eat. But the golden age gave way to silver, silver to brass and, as evil grows on earth, brass gives way to iron:

> modesty and truth and faith fled the earth, and in their place came tricks and plots and snares, violence and cursed love of gain. Men now spread sails to the winds . . . and keels of pine . . . leaps insolently over unknown waves. Not only did men demand of the bounteous fields the crops and sustenance they owed, but they delved as well into the very bowels of the earth; and the wealth which the creator had hidden away . . . was brought to light, wealth that pricks men on to crime. (*Metamorphoses*, Book i, trans. Frank Justus Miller, Loeb Classical Library, 1916, pp. 11–13).

Money was the root of evil in the Graeco-Roman as well as the
Judaeo-Christian world; and man, ceasing to be content with
the pleasures earth naturally affords, falls from innocence in his
quest for wealth.

Volpone slily congratulates himself on not doing what
wicked men do! But we cannot believe him, and if we do
Mosca's complimentary speech should warn us. What Mosca
says is that Volpone does not hurt anyone who is weak and
vulnerable; his clients are, in fact, all wealthy and intelligent
enough to protect themselves. But Mosca says this in such
hyperbolic language that we expect any intelligent master to
see through it. Volpone agrees with what Mosca says (confirm-
ing our suspicions of the characters of both), and Mosca
launches on an even more exaggerated piece of flattery.
Volpone is no miser, he enjoys his wealth and shares it with
others. This is all gift-wrapped with references and comparisons until Mosca gets to the point, and is rewarded with money.

Volpone's uncommon way of getting money prepares us for
the arrival of the carrion-eating birds. But before that we see
how the absence of normal ties or social responsibilities leaves
Volpone with nothing else to do but 'cocker up my genius, and
live free' [I i 71]. We must then ask what that freedom amounts
to. The arrival, in scene ii, of his dwarf, eunuch and
hermaphrodite fool is startling; they present us with a vision of
Volpone's world. They are human beings in whom the natural
order has been unbalanced, emblems of what this new world
can produce. Volpone lives for pleasure and the masque is his
pleasure. It is not very entertaining for us (indeed, when
Volpone is not acting a role, he seems to live life on a very
limited level – which is probably Jonson's point). Remove the
spiritual, ethical and moral dimensions and what money can
buy is remarkably finite. The masque performed by these three
grotesques takes as its theme the transmigration of souls,
blurring the distinctions usually maintained between god, man
and beast. The verse is bad enough to suggest burlesque, and
the long history of the soul which came from Apollo to end up in
a hermaphrodite fool shows how the great wealth and wisdom
of the classical past has shrunk to the age of Volpone. The
masque is dreadful, but who finds it to his taste? Volpone! The
whole play that follows can be seen as a perversion of

Renaissance culture, aspirations, civilisation. As if to prove the point the birds of prey arrive.

Herford and the Simpsons have been criticised for complaining the Jonson 'transfigures avarice with the glamour of religion and idealism'. They miss the irony but perhaps we should take their view into account. The speeches are meant to be attractive, we are supposed to be attracted. This grandeur (however spurious), this joy in living (however badly), and Mosca's sharp manipulation of the self-centred Volpone, contrast dramatically with the poverty of spirit, judgement and imagination shown by the clients. Our pleasure makes us accomplices. Volpone and Mosca between them make a splendid passionate pair (though most of Volpone's performances have to do with death, disease or decay) and Volpone has the genius (i.e., the essential spirit) to live free to all the delights that fortune calls him to and wealth can buy; he is ingenious, larger-than-life, theatrical, and he speaks in good resounding verse. As with Doctor Faustus, delight turns out to be worth not very much. But we still respond to their mastery (and the mountebank scene shows how well they can perform) even as our unease deepens. The arrival of Celia should remove any doubts about that unease.

The Wooing of Celia: III vii 140–267
The placing of this event is a good example of how Jonson uses his plot. In Act III scene i, Mosca is excessively pleased with his own abilities, only to be confronted by a contemptuous if stupid Bonario [III ii] whom he persuades of his honesty and then reveals that the young man is to be disinherited by Corbaccio. Arriving back at Volpone's palazzo, Mosca finds he has to get rid of Lady Would-be. Having achieved that, he has just got Bonario concealed when Corvino instead of Corbaccio arrives, with Celia. So Bonario has to be moved out into the gallery where he can hear nothing. But Bonario is once more suspicious. He may not stay where Mosca has put him. Or, if he does, he may still not be out of ear-shot – for, by the end of the scene with Celia, Volpone, frustrated by his lack of his success with her, must be getting louder and louder, so that the whole of Venice can hear him! At any rate, we know that Bonario is waiting in the wings.

Some decision must be made on the importance of III i in the light of what happens. Volpone rejoices less in the 'glad possession' than in the 'cunning purchase', but we do not overlook either 'glad' or 'possession'. Mainly it is the game, the sport, that keeps Volpone happy, and this particular game is growing stale. Celia is a new diversion. Mosca does not plan what happens though when an opportunity is offered (as in Act v) he seizes it as the rules of the game allow. The trick is always to keep the various characters separate until the first Court scene where the master-trick is to get them all to work together. In the Celia scene Mosca's planning is spoiled by the eagerness with which Corvino turns up to hand his wife over to Volpone. Celia, from the beginning of the play, is offered in terms of gold and silver rather than flesh and blood. Given the world of the play, she ought to present no problem: she is cleverly acquired and ought to be easily enjoyed. Volpone simply cannot believe that there is a human being who is not infected by the disease. His inability to grasp this feeds his mounting frustration, and the fact that he hears only what he wants to hear (as in the interchange with Mosca in Act I) explains his use of force when words, amazingly, fail. Splendid though his bedroom scenes are, they do limit Volpone. But in the mountebank scene he has shown us how he can charm with words. Celia is impressed by his performance in St Mark's Square since she drops her handkerchief. Sir Politick is also impressed and his admiration should qualify ours.

Moreover, glad possession of Celia rather than cunning purchase puts Volpone in the same position as the suitors and renders him as vulnerable as they are. His language here is doubly inappropriate: to the role he is playing, and to the situation in which he is playing that role. Celia is mainly silent (but audiences accustomed to Beckett and Pinter will know the value of silence), and when she speaks what she says is memorable in the wrong sort of way. But her silence is not surprising. A jealous husband, who recently has been dragging her up and down the room and threatening her with a chastity belt for dropping a handerchief out of the window, is suddenly transformed into a pander. She is thrust into a room with a dying old man who is suddenly transformed into a viril lusty lover. Both Bonario and Celia are alien elements here. Bonario, the good one, can be fooled by a few tears and some words into believing that Mosca is honest; Celia is constantly associated in deed and imagery with a Christian attitude. Neither character uses language except in an ordinary honest way which, on stage, means that what they say lacks dramatic force. But it also suggests to us that language is being splendidly *abused* by the other characters.

Volpone opens his seduction with a song ('Come, my Celia, let us prove'). A romantic Volpone is something new and an actor who can sing pleasantly (e.g., Paul Scofield) is needed here. Donald Wolfit tried doing the song as a recitative and mimed to a guitar played off-stage, which was comic in quite the wrong way. The song is adapted from the fifth Ode of Catullus and explores the conventional *carpe diem* theme – though 'sports' [III vii 166] might recall the use of that word when Volpone called for his household pets; and the sun, too, could take us back to Act I. The song is also one of three written about that time, presumably to Cecelia Bulstrode, of which the best known is 'Drink to me, only, with thine eyes'. Celia's response is not encouraging. Not for the last time does she wish her beauty destroyed if it is to cause this sort of behaviour. What kind of woman (or girl?) is Celia? The Court returns her at the end of the play to her father with her dowry trebled which might suggest either that the marriage has not yet been consummated (such contracts with young girls were not unusual), or that as 'damaged goods' she will need a larger dowry to get another husband. Certainly, if not a virgin she is innocent of the kinds of sexual sophistication that Volpone offers. On the other hand, she speaks quietly but firmly, and the earlier episode with the handkerchief allows an actress to give the role an element of fun and spirit. Here she must be seen as stunned and bewildered and conventional.

Volpone, of course, cannot believe that this piety and respectability are anything more than a disguise beneath which the true Celia hides, and he proceeds to offer the things that will bring out that real person. The feast is, not unexpectedly, one of drinking jewels, associated in rapid succession with Cleopatra, St Mark and Lollia Paulina. St Mark reminds us that this is Venice, but he sits with splendid awkwardness between two ladies whose reputation leaves much to be desired. Cleopatra's

fondness for luxury and lewdness (not to mention her political
cunning) is still well known, largely thanks to Shakespeare, and
Jonson's audience would have recognised Lollia Paulina, the
wife of Caligula and the daughter of an extortioner whose
personal wealth was enormous and who appeared at a
betrothal feast glittering like the sun under her jewels. Drinking
and losing jewels leads to food which, once more, is a matter of
ransacking the world for the rare and the difficult (regardless of
edibility or taste) and culminating in the threat to destroy the
fabulous and unique Phoenix. This is good heady stuff, but if
we listen carefully we discover that it is nothing more than a
hymn in praise of waste. Again Celia's answer is brief and
precise. She starts with the words 'good sir' and contrasts mind
and innocence with delight and wealth. She defines her view of
wealth, rejecting (with acute perception) 'sensual baits' and
ending with 'conscience'. The argument may be ridiculous,
even comical, in context but that is the fault of the context.

Volpone dismisses conscience as the beggar's virtue and
plunges on into further excesses. Gold and amber (used in
cooking and medicine) are to be drunk and alluring prospects
are envisaged: after an opulent bath Celia is to sit in the middle
of an antic with the household poets before she and Volpone
make love in all the shapes drawn from Ovid's *Metamorphoses*.
And when they weary of playing at gods they will change into
more modern situations. It is all very exciting but concentrates
on costumes rather than any relationship (or even sex), and
Volpone ends with the idea of tranfusing their wandering souls.
He claims that Celia's beauty has transformed him into a
young and ardent lover, and those wandering souls specifically
recall the tale told in the masque in Act I. Volpone and Celia
will assume as many shapes as that original soul did and, by
implication, end up in a foolish monster.

Endless pleasure means, for Volpone, endless change: even
in love Volpone cannot sit still or be himself. Amid all this
passionate excitement Celia should, surely, remain still and be
herself: bemused, frightened but rational. Some critics (e.g.
Dutton) have asked which would have faltered first if Bonario
had not intervened: Volpone's ego or Celia's virtue. But Jonson
answers that question when he makes Volpone resort to force.
Celia responds to all this baroque nonsense with an argument.

Her speech does not read well, but it could be delivered well; and, by contrast with Volpone's habit of free association and increasing extravagance, Celia's careful assessment of the situation (using words like 'saints', 'heaven' and 'heart') offers an alternative: be merciful if you are a human being (and have ears, eyes and a heart) and release me, or, since the loss of my honour is death, kill me immediately, or be more of a man and change your lust to wrath and ruin my beauty so that it no longer tempts you. The appeal is not simply to religion but to Volpone as a human being. Though she is unclean, a leper, she will pray for him hourly and tell the world that he is virtuous. Such language is unthinkable in Volpone's bedroom and the only word he seems to grasp is 'virtuous' [III vii 259] which he assumes is her coy way of finding out if he is impotent or not. He translates the whole matter of her prayer into a joke about a hernia, albeit a classical hernia. The magic of words having failed, he resorts to force – at which point Bonario enters to meet force with force.

Bonario's opening words [III vii 267] are not impressive, and the sight of a young man with a drawn sword can hardly be other than comic at this juncture. But again the conventional looks foolish only to test our values. Bonario's words reduce Volpone's great sensual aria to what it really is: gold is dross, Volpone's god an idol and this splendid chamber the den of a fox. Such clear vision and precise language are, however, unavailing in Volpone's world, as the subsequent court scene shows.

PART TWO: PERFORMANCE

8 INTRODUCTION

Since the basis of a play is disguise, a play about disguises should be popular. *Volpone* was an immediate success; very possibly Burbage, who was certainly in the cast, played the title-role. The staging of the play is fairly simple – and indeed it had to be, since it was performed at The Globe, then under more *ad hoc* circumstances at Cambridge and Oxford (whether in college halls or, as has been argued, in one of the local inns), and at court. The production requires a curtained area, where Bonario can be temporarily hidden and Volpone can spy on the legacy-hunters, and an upper gallery to which Bonario is directed (though he may not go there) and which can also serve as the balcony to Celia's chamber in the mounteback scene. Apart from the need for a large crowd in that scene in Act II (and only there), there is but one scene that presents any difficulty in its staging: Act v scene xi. Here Volpone's encounter with Nano, Androgyno and Castrone interrupts the final courtroom episode. This may have been added as an after-thought. Rather than clear the stage for this brief interlude only to reassemble the Court, it seems likely that in the original production Act v sc. xi would have been played in front of the courtroom scenario, with the action and the actors in the latter 'arrested'. This is not inconsistent with the devices of the period; and it was used successfully by Sir Tyrone Guthrie, for example, in his 1964 and 1968 productions.

The play was revived promptly for the reopened theatre after the Restoration (1660) and was one of the three Jonson comedies to hold the stage, though its realism became more and more outdated, and the disadvantageous comparison with Shakespeare grew stronger. (Cf. R. G. Noyes, *Ben Jonson on the English Stage*, 1935.) Like the plays of Shakespeare, *Volpone* was presented in altered form. In Jonson's case the alterations were mainly in the form of reduction, since then (as now) his plays were felt to be overlong for a theatre that decreed that a comedy should last no longer than two hours. This left time for an afterpiece, with or without divertissements of music and dancing. Jeremy Collier*, who was no friend to the English playhouse, found *Volpone* morally irreproachable – though someone certainly tried to suppress a production of it in 1700, and critical opinion as well as stage practice led to a revision which generally aimed at the elimination of unnecessary characters (the Would-be couple and Peregrine), the removal of the mountebank and the tortoise shell scenes, and a great deal of rewriting to purge the dialogue of its disgusting frankness. The dwarf, eunuch and hermaphrodite were reduced as far as possible, and the Renaissance spirit of the play was banished in favour of an approach more suitable to the manner of the time. After its revival in 1785, it dropped out of the repertoire until 1921.

Since Jonson always felt that his own age did not appreciate him, and sought therefore to appeal to posterity with versions of his plays carefully printed to prevent actors taking liberties, he would have been dismayed by both the adapted versions and his declining reputation. But he would not have been surprised by either. The general intention of all the adaptations was, as David McPherson suggests, to transform a very unconventional comedy into a more conventional one. (Cf. his 'Rough Beast into Tame Fox', *Studies in the Literary Imagination*, VI, no. 1, 1973.) For example, the version of 1771 by George Colman (the elder) did not tamper with the main plot, but it did expurgate the text to remove all language that was too violent, erotic, nasty or blasphemous – thus earning praise from one reviewer (in the *Theatrical Review**) for offering the public a comedy that was now suitable 'to the professed chastity of the present age'. Even in bowdlerised form, however, *Volpone* did not survive beyond 1785, and for the next 135 years was not played in England.

The most notable version in the eighteenth century was Ludwig Tieck's free adaptation in German of 1793 which sought to tame the Fox and reduce the play to the currently popular form of sentimental drama. It was this version which Coleridge clearly had in mind when he offered his suggestions

---

* As noted at the outset of Part One, an asterisk is used to signalise authors and critics whose work is excerpted in the Casebook on *Volpone*, edited by Jonas A. Barish.

for 'improving' *Volpone*. As was noted in section 2, above, Tieck's *Herr Von Fuchs* makes Celia the ward of Corvino and Bonario her lover – and the lovers triumph at the end.)

The most significant adaptation of the play was the more recent version by Stefan Zweig performed in Germany in 1926. Here Zweig solved the problem of the ending by making Mosca the hero. This version enjoyed an astonishing success. It was adapted for the stage by Jules Romains in France and formed the basis for Maurice Tourneur's film *Volpone*, in which Mosca was played by the great Louis Jouvet. Ruth Langner translated the play back into English and her version was first produced on Broadway in 1928. Zweig removes the subplot altogether replacing Lady Would-be with a courtesan called Canina who is Volpone's mistress. The poetry goes completely, of course, and so does Volpone's household, which now consists only of a few grooms and musicians. Mosca is described as a gad-fly, listed as Volpone's toady and is a Venetian, 'a gay, vivacious fellow', who has been in his patron's service for only eight weeks since he rescued him from a debtors' prison. Celia is renamed Colomba, while Bonario is a sea-captain, 'big, brusque, loud, clanking his sword, extravagantly military' – and now called, rather obviously, Leone. The most crucial change, however, is that Zweig turns Volpone into a rich Levantine from Smyrna, which makes him vulnerable in Venice. The only touch of Jonsonian humour in the whole play comes at the moment when Volpone throws off his disguise and is revealed as healthy and virile. This the pious Colomba takes to be a miracle granted by the Madonna.

Zweig has avoided the obvious solution (to make Celia and Bonario lovers and the hero and heroine) by turning Mosca into the hero of the play. His aim is to set the gold free, to give it wings – at which, considering where Volpone found him, he is probably very good. He rationalises the function of parasites by saying that their role is to spread wealth, which he seems to regard as a kind of fertilizer. Jonson's Mosca is intelligent, devious and an opportunist who miscalculates only in the last scenes what his master is capable of. But Zweig's Mosca from the beginning wants his master to relax and enjoy himself rather than devise new plots and stratagems. When this Mosca is made heir he promises to return everything Volpone has

extracted from the suitors, and invites them all to a feast paid
for by himself (presumably with Volpone's money?), while
Volpone flees to Genoa where he has a ship full of loot. Mosca,
therefore, ends the play on a note of gaiety. The money is all
back in circulation, and a feast is almost as good as a wedding
at the end of a comedy. Although this is a Venice where judges
can neither be bought nor fooled, no one is punished and the
young triumph over the old – which, again, is a traditional end
to a comedy.

In all this talk of liberating wealth and spreading it around,
there are rumblings of Marxist thought. Volpone and the
legacy-hunters are the inevitable products of an evil capitalist
society. Yet Zweig makes it clear that what he wants is a romp
in the style of the *commedia dell'arte*. His stage directions ask that
the play should be acted 'lightly, quickly, caricatured rather
than realistic, *allegro con brio*'. Edmund Wilson in 1928 saw this
version (in Langner's translation) as an improvement on the
original play because the gold was liberated and 'to everyone's
relief Mosca flings it about the stage in fistfuls'. Presumably
Mosca will soon be back where he came from. This festive
ending was certainly a drastic avoidance of the implacability
which makes Jonson's version so impressive, and Eric Bentley
is, I think, correct in suggesting that a great play has been
ruined. For example, this (as seen by Bentley) Mosca is
unintelligible:

> The adaptors seem forever on the brink of releasing some secret
> about him. It was Jouvet's achievement [*in the film version*] to
> conceal the fact that they had no secret to release. This Mosca
> always seemed to be having his own thoughts, and even misgivings,
> though actually all that was involved was that Zweig and Romains
> couldn't take Ben Jonson's moral severity. They wished to be
> sophisticated and replace the accusing finger by a shrug of the
> shoulders. Though the worse villain, Volpone, is bundled off into
> beggery, the lesser one, Mosca, remains to enjoy perpetual
> carnival. This surely is Viennese whipped cream instead of the full
> Mermaid wine, Parisian pinchbeck instead of Jonsonian
> gold. (*What is Theatre*, 1969, pp. 368–9.)

Few seemed to notice, moreover, the irony of a successful play
that was translated from the German into English when the
original was already available in English. What is more, a

version of Zweig's German play – translated into French and
thence rendered into Hungarian, from which language it was
transmuted into English by George Mikes – was the inaugural
production at the Billingham Forum Theatre in 1963! Ruth
Langner's version subsequently underwent adaptation in
America by Edward Parone, who moved the whole action to
the San Francisco of 1872.

Volpone has been the source for a German opera with music
by Francis Burt (1960), an English opera with music by
Malcolm Williamson (1964), a musical comedy (*Foxy*, set in the
Yukon gold rush and starring Bert Lahr, which opened the
Dawson City Festival in 1962 and moved to Broadway in
1964), and a very free film version, *The Honeypot* (1966),
adapted by Jo Mankiewicz from the play by Frederick Knott
called *Mr Fox of Venice* (1959).

Happily, after a gap of 135 years, the original play was
revived for two performances by the Phoenix Society in 1921 at
the Lyric Theatre, Hammersmith. This production was
described by T. S. Eliot, with some justice, as 'the most
important theatrical event of the year in London' (*Dial*, LXX,
June 1921). Since that time R. B. Parker has listed at least 35
professional productions by the quatercentennial year of 1972
('*Volpone* in Performance: 1921–72', *Renaissance Drama*, n.s. IX,
1978).

The problem is always one of softening the play. Thus, the
classic production by Charles Dullin in 1928 showed little trace
of Jonson's moral fervour. In this French interpretation
monsters were changed into gulls, and buffoons mocked by the
director with mischievous enjoyment. Dullin transformed
Jonson's savage humour into light-hearted satire in a setting of
suitably bright sharp colours: an approach which made him
much more at home in Restoration comedies. In England, the
driving force in restoring the play was almost certainly Donald
Wolfit.

9   WOLFIT'S INTERPRETATION: PRODUCTIONS OF 1938 AND
1940–53

Sir Donald Wolfit (he was knighted in 1957) has some claim to being regarded as the finest Volpone of our time. He is at least the yardstick by which subsequent performances tend to be measured.[1] His biographer Ronald Harwood describes his performance as one of the actor's most magnificent creations and finest comic display:

> It was a luxurious performance. No actor then alive could portray a character's relish in his own evil better than Wolfit. When Volpone laughed it was, as Joseph Chelton described it, 'gloriously diabolical, right down from the bowels of Hell and up into Jupiter's anteroom'. Sensuality took on a religious significance in Volpone's bedchamber; when Wolfit's Fox touched silks or fingered a jewel, or sipped a heady wine, it was in the nature of an unholy communion.   (*Sir Donald Wolfit: His Life and Work in the Unfashionable Theatre*, 1971.)

Harwood (p. 156) quotes John Mayes on the scene with Celia where Wolfit 'makes himself known as a vigorous, lusty Croesus with the imagination of a poet and the proclivities of a satyr', and which showed his 'marvellous range and command of vocal technique':

> His hypnotic, chuckling laugh as he faced his Celia was an extraordinarily powerful moment, and an audience waited, completely controlled, not knowing which way the fox would jump, and then came the frightening, slow pacing walk towards his victim followed by another soaring speech of verse splendours

Not every critic admired Wolfit's verse delivery. Kenneth Tynan (who was not Wolfit's favourite critic!) described listening to the actor speaking verse as rather like 'watching a rebellious rogue elephant walking a tightrope. It is enjoyable because it is very, very strange. Like a prize-fighter nursing a young flower . . . so is Mr Wolfit when a line of poetry is delivered into his hands' (*He That Plays The King*, 1950, p. 85). Nevertheless Tynan admired Wolfit's stage presence:

> There has never been an actor of greater gusto than Wolfit: he has dynamism, energy, bulk and stature, and he joins these together with a sheer relish for resonant words which splits small theatres as Caruso shattered wine-glasses.   (Ibid., p. 40.)

---

1. See R. B. Parker, 'Wolfit's Fox: An Interpretation of *Volpone*', *University of Toronto Quarterly*, XLV, no. 3 (1976), pp. 200–20.

Tynan listed Wolfit's Lear as one of the best dozen performances he has seen between 1944–8 and his Volpone as one of
the four memorable performances ever given by Wolfit: 'a solid
caricature overflowing with bourgeois wickedness'. R. B.
Parker writes of great vocal control and variety, and a feeling
for poetry, but concedes that this sometimes produced 'a rather
self-consciously "beautiful" speaking style'. I suspect this is
what audiences then wanted and that it is only present-day
audiences, used to the mumble and chatter of television, who
would feel this as too premeditatedly 'beautiful'. The self-
conscious quality of Wolfit's delivery was entirely suited to his
Volpone, who spoke the words as if he were caressing them 'like
objets d'art'. Tynan spoke of its 'frightening, dilapidated whin-
ing note' when Volpone was angry: a tone Wolfit exploited
thoroughly when frustrated by the arrival of Bonario or in the
final court scene. In a symposium on Jonson (*Gambit*, 6, no. 22,
Jan. 1973) both Terry Hands and Colin Blakely agreed that
Volpone was one of his greatest performances because Wolfit
had 'the courage to be malevolent' and was himself a giant
eccentric: 'And the men that Jonson writes about are giant
eccentrics. Monsters.'

Wolfit was first asked to play Volpone in 1938 in a
production at the Westminster Theatre directed by Michael
Macowan; this was the first public performance of *Volpone* in
London for over 150 years. In his autobiography *First Interval*
(1954), Wolfit described this as a swift and colourful production designed by Peter Goffin with some 'very curious music'
composed by Edmund Rubbra. James Agate* observed of this
music that it conjured from the throats of clarinet, oboe and
bassoon 'a concourse of sounds even more obnoxious . . . than
the scenes they accompany' and Wolfit recalled that in this
production:

> The bitter savagery of Jonson was stressed and the broad gusty
> humour which disarms the nastiness of the theme was to some
> extent lacking, but it pleased a highly sophisticated audience and
> ran for six weeks. I was to discover later when I added the play to
> my repertoire that it could be played to please audiences every-
> where and that a simpler treatment was equally effective.

This simpler treatment took shape in 1940 when Maynard

Keynes, then Bursar of King's College, Cambridge, invited Wolfit to prepare four plays for the Cambridge Arts Festival. Wolfit not only played the title-part but also directed and designed the production, roles which he never relinquished. Reviving *Volpone* gave him great pleasure and he sought to discover that 'greaty gusty laughter of Jonson which disarmed the nastiness of the theme'. The University audience 'took every point'. At Keynes's suggestion he used a Cambridge don, Donald Beves, to play the role of Lady Politick Would-be who was 'an excellent female impersonator in the real Elizabethan sense'. It is fairly certain that this role was, in fact, played by a man and not a boy in Jonson's time. It was basically this production which Wolfit revived in 1942, 1944, 1947 and 1953, taking it on tour to the provinces, Canada, the United States of America and Egypt. Wolfit's last appearance as Volpone was in a television version for the BBC's 'World Theatre' series in 1959, directed by Stephen Harrison. If only a faint echo of Wolfit's stage performance, it at least survives in the archives.

The first question a director has to ask when presenting *Volpone* to a modern audience is probably: what should it look like? The stage could be fairly bare (recalling what we imagine Elizabethan staging was like); or the designer (mindful that this is a Jacobean play) could try to capture the Venetian setting to emphasise the greed and materialism of the play; or the whole play could be transposed into another, possibly contemporary, period. The most radical form of this last idea was Joan Littlewood's production at Stratford East in 1955, where Mosca entered on a bicycle and Sir Politick hid in a frogman's suit instead of a tortoise shell and left the stage by diving into the orchestra pit. It must be admitted that the play was useful to Littlewood, who did it with immense relish and much comic invention as a satire on greed and graft in modern society. Peter Goffin's set for the Macowan–Wolfit production of 1938 was, in James Agate's words, 'a gold-encrusted Jacobean tableau which Mr Sickert ought to paint'. The design for Act I survives and shows that the basic colour was magenta with arches at the side and back which focus attention on a large bed-shrine under a twinkling sky.

Wolfit's own self-made productions were, by contrast, of the kind usually blamed on William Poel (1854–1934) with whom

Wolfit had worked and whom he admired tremendously. Poel had reintroduced the Elizabethan method of staging, using sixteenth-century costumes, as few props as possible and an area for acting set in curtains which was roughly approximate to what the Elizabethans used. Wolfit's presentation was very much a touring production and this, as much as reverence for the theories of Poel, may account for what he did. Parker points out that a floor cloth of large black and white lozenges gave the 'Venetian' effect for the play; Volpone's bedroom was built with flats of golden brown and red drapes, with a large four-poster bed on a dais at centre-back. The courtroom scenes used much the same flats but draped in black; minor scenes were played before a traverse curtain or the front curtains, with the lighting concentrated on that area. Simple and effective at first, it grew to seem old-fashioned and, with frequent touring, shabby. Wolfit's designer was Ernest Stern, who had worked for Max Reinhardt in such spectacular productions as *The Miracle*, but he seems to have adapted easily to the demands of a poor touring company. By 1953, as Parker observes, *The Stage* was complaining about the demands of the play (opulence, grandeur, movement, easy continuity) as contrasted with a set that was not luxurious, shaking walls and a 'clumsy and crudely-lit attempt at realism'. Wolfit, in fact, seems to have had very little visual sense, and though his wife, the actress Rosalind Iden (herself a painter), tried to point this out to him, he never did see it. And in many ways it did not matter. Richard Burton recalls a performance of *King Lear*:

> Sir Donald's sets were not made by the best craftsmen and in the second performance the set fell in; and out of this enormous rubbish came the towering figure of Sir Donald pushing the set up and holding it up; and he looked as big a man as I've ever seen in my life. And I've worked for some very big men. (*Listener*, 18 April 1968, p. 501.)

Props and costumes came in for the same criticism. Wolfit's productions were centred on himself in the tradition of Irving and other great actor–managers, and what was good enough for Irving was good enough for him. He was necessarily careful (in those unsubsidised days) of wasting money on costumes or sets: his props were glass and paste, and his gold was painted wood.

Parker recalls two props of interest. The first was the chastity belt [II ii] designed for Macowan's 1938 production by Una Ellis-Fermor: an ugly hoop wrapped in surgical bandages, which tells us more than a thousand words about Corvino's nasty character. And the other a large 'pearl', one of Corvino's gifts [I iv] which Wolfit used to pop into his mouth when Corvino wanted it back, only to spit it out laughing when Corvino had gone. At one performance he swallowed the pearl accidentally, almost choking before it was recovered.

On the actor's costume, Parker tells us:

> Wolfit's Volpone combined the beast and the dandy: [he] wore a long red wig swept back behind the ears and over the collar, curled red mustachios, Mephistophelian eyebrows, and a divided red beard.

A long black robe with fox-fur collar was worn over a white shirt, yellow tights and with pointed red shoes. A single ear-ring completed the picture. For the invalid he wore ear-flaps, a scarf and a shawl; for Scoto he wore a Guy Fawkes hat and a black eye-patch. The Celia in the Macowan production had been played by Rachel Kempson – tall, dark and aristocratic – a piece of casting that Macowan disliked and which Wolfit subsequently avoided; both directors seemed to feel that Celia should be plump, luscious and blond, and Wolfit was able to use Rosalind Iden in the role, wearing a pink dress that set off her golden hair. She was to be submissive and young – the kind of girl who arouses lust in big men (and the Corvinos were always big in Wolfit's productions). Wolfit seems to have had fixed notions about character: good characters wore blue and should be blond, while bad characters wore black and were ravenhaired! Rosaline Iden was exactly right as Celia, completely innocent and rousing both her jealous husband and Volpone to violent anger.

When Wolfit began to play Volpone he was trim and athletic; his Fox was a man in early middle age, a man in his prime for whom senility is a genuine acting challenge. Volpone's actual age is vague but most actors have followed Wolfit's lead in this. As time passed, however, Wolfit developed a paunch. This was brilliantly incorporated into the performance – the lolling figure with a belly and slender legs summing up a life passed in pleasure and being paid for. He saw Volpone as tremendously virile and sexually potent with a greed for life that imposed itself on the world around him. The cruel streak, the sinister side of Volpone, he probably got from Wilfrid Lawson's performance for Sir Barry Jackson's Birmingham Repertory Theatre in 1935, and from Macowan's 1938 interpretation of the play. But his aim was always to 'disarm' the nastiness of the play by comic gusto – a word he uses frequently to describe the spirit of the role.

In the Macowan production the three freaks had been presented as part of the savage atmosphere: Nano was red-haired (to strengthen the view that they were Volpone's bastards), Castrone was a mute in harem costume, while Androgyno had one side dressed like a man and the other like a woman, and was instructed to act as far as possible in profile. The dance mime in Macowan's interpretation was extremely disturbing. Wolfit replaced this with a chorus-girl dance choreographed by Rosalind Iden which trivialised the freaks. Volpone was not amused by them, not even by the badness of their performance. The prompt books refer to these three characters bleakly as the 'queers', and Wolfit's attitude to them on (as off) stage was contemptuous. They were decidedly in terror of his contempt, emphasising the sadistic undertones to Wolfit's performance. Nevertheless Wolfit tried to keep them more comic than sordid as part of his policy to present the play as a comedy. In this his performance as Scoto, a huckster with a Nottinghamshire accent, played a large part. But the underlying sadism explains why Volpone decides to play the last trick (in Act v), and Wolfit watched the humiliation of his dupes with great glee from behind the curtains. And even in the mountebank scene he stressed the sexual side of Volpone in order to strengthen the scene with Celia. She is not yielding to him there but he *is* sexually powerful. Rather she was simply in a daze, mesmerised by the power of the onslaught. Wolfit had played Svengali on film and his Volpone 'paralysed Celia as a stoat can do a rabbit, moving constantly towards and away from her . . .' (Parker, p. 213). Indeed in 1947 Wolfit actually made Svengali-like passes with his hands before her, eliciting a rebuke from *The Times* (10 April 1947) that it was one thing to make a pass at a girl and quite another to make passes. At the end Celia gabbled off her plea to heaven while Wolfit paced very slowly towards her, chuckling and contemptuous. At the point of rescue his frustration was literally held at bay only by the drawn sword, and his pent-up anger was released on poor Mosca in the next scene.

One hardly need mention Mosca in Wolfit's productions. No other luminary could (or be allowed to) shine near the sun. Sir Tyrone Guthrie remembered vividly Wolfit's performance as Tamburlaine but it was a solo *tour de force*; which was the problem because the English theatre was moving into a period of ensemble play. Too often, as Guthrie points out, 'he was the particular bright star and head of a comet of which the tail became a little fuzzy' (*Listener*, 18 April 1968, p. 501). This led to his inability to collaborate with others, but it was also his strength. He is remarkable for solo roles that suited his temperament, and Volpone did just that. Parker describes him as an extraordinary man: 'a natural athlete with boundless energy and self-confidence and a fierce, sometimes almost paranoid, sense of competition' (p. 202). The dark side, the destructive element, the need to feel superior, may have led to quarrels with eminent collaborators like Guthrie, but they suited his interpretation of Volpone. In the tradition of actor–managers, Wolfit ran his company with autocratic selfishness (again suitable to one view of Volpone), which led to the legend that he surrounded himself with actors who would not challenge his supremacy. The facts behind this do not entirely substantiate the legend, but tales of backstage terror and harassment of particular actors are too numerous to be merely fiction. His actors (and his audiences) were always treated like children who must obey – though this in the case of the audience led to a terrifyingly personal relationship with every member in the auditorium. Economics played some part in the choice of actors he could afford and loyalty to long-standing members of the troupe who should perhaps have been dismissed. It is true, however, he only took particular care with his own speeches, and his general instruction to the other actors was speed and more speed. Parker has argued, plausibly, that this trick (making the others speak fast so that the star could draw attention to himself by speaking slowly) had some point in *Volpone*, contrasting as it did the farcical action with all its intrigues with the poetic musings of Volpone himself. Wolfit when required (as in the mountebank scene) could speak very fast himself, and in the seduction scene he ranged from slow persuasion to a torrent of promises. And, of course, in a touring production the length of performance is crucial, and speed was needed to get the play over by the time for the last bus.

Mosca, in fact, is the only challenge to Volpone's superior and central position. In the Macowan production, Alan Wheatley chose to be, in James Agate's words*, 'a silk thread among the hempen villainy', an independent intriguer from the start whose bid to take over in Act v comes as no surprise. According to Macowan, Wolfit was not pleased by this and in his own production Mosca was not allowed to be too prominent. Wolfit invariably cast light-voiced and clean-shaven actors for the role, cut many of the asides and added business to keep Volpone as the centre of attention even when Jonson allowed Mosca to be dominant. The scene one most clearly remembers in this respect is Act I where, from the moment an orange beard followed by a night-cap emerged from the bed-curtains to say 'Good Morning', Wolfit held the stage. He applied his own make-up and costumes, and entered into the role of the invalid with enormous energy. Even when hidden in the bed his feet wriggled with such glee beneath the coverlets as Mosca made fools of the legacy hunters that it was difficult to take notice of anything else on the stage. Mosca's soliloquy, which could not be cut, was delivered with the actor leaning against the proscenium arch, plucking petals from a flower while scene changes took place, noisily, behind the curtains. A bland Mosca suited Wolfit, and the idea of treachery comes to the parasite only at the last possible moment, when Volpone makes him his heir. Wolfit treated his Mosca with the same harshness as he meted out to the freaks and, again in Act I, there was never the slightest suggestion that he was taken in by or even liked Mosca's flattery.

The text, therefore, was ruthlessly pruned to remove any possibility that the audience might laugh *at* Volpone rather than *with* him. Apart from the reduction of Mosca's role and the usual pruning of classical allusions, the main cut concerned the Politick Would-be pair; always an embarrassment! Macowan deleted the Would-be subplot completely, remarking in his 1938 programme note that such satires on common Elizabethan types, if relevant in Jonson's time, were quite out of keeping with 'the atmosphere of macabre farce and passionate hatred which inspire the rest of the play'. Wolfit restored the subplot for the 1940 Cambridge revival. Lady Would-be appears in the programmes for 1942 and 1944 (when she was again played by a man – though not, as in 1940, by a Cambridge don!). But the part appears to have been cut on the 1944 tour at least, since reviewers remark on its absence. Wolfit seems never to have known what to do with the eccentric English lady, perhaps because she really reduces Volpone to helplessness and shows him in a ridiculous light. The subplot was never entirely removed, though the feud between Peregrine and Sir Politick was, which successfully eliminated the tortoise scene.

Wolfit's treatment of the ending remains a classic. At times he toyed with the idea of playing the Avocatori as farce. They appeared dressed identically in skull caps and horn-rimmed spectacles (reminiscent of Macowan's production, where they resembled owls), and they moved in unison like puppets, throwing their papers around in confusion. This horseplay sometimes got out of hand and was much criticised. Here again Wolfit was trying to 'disarm' the nastiness which had pleased 'sophisticated' audiences in 1938. *Volpone* remained an unconventional comedy. Wolfit's howl when the Court passed sentence upon him, rising to a prolonged stress on the last sibilant in 'Fox' [v xii 125], the hands palm outwards over the eyes, was striking and serious. Its aweful effect was then lessened by the comedy of sentencing the lesser rogues by a judiciary that was itself ridiculous, both balancing Volpone's lofty rage. Then Wolfit gathered all the tones and moods together in the epilogue, which he delivered as an actor. The audience could see the man beneath the make-up begging the audience for applause (in one of his hanging-from-the-curtain style postures) but still using the Volpone voice. Thus Volpone's failure in the action of the play became Wolfit's success in the performance of the play: actor and role stood side by side.

Wolfit's performance was by no means definitive, and his production certainly was not. But he captured two essential things about the character: his dual nature and his fondness for acting – and to both he was temperamentally suited. He could, as Harold Pinter observes 'tear the guts out of you'.

10   RALPH RICHARDSON: GEORGE DEVINE'S PRODUCTION, 1952

The 1952 production at Stratford was remarkable for two things: the set and Sir Ralph Richardson's idiosyncratic interpretation of Volpone. Alan Dent (*News Chronicle*, 16 July) suggested that the stage looked like paintings by Longhi, and this is probably the most elaborate example of staging the play to recall the Renaissance and Venice in all its opulence. *Volpone* was George Devine's first production at Stratford and the choice of a non-Shakespearean play was his. It had been a long time since audiences at the Memorial Theatre had seen a play by anyone other than Shakespeare.

For this production Devine mobilised all the stage machinery installed in the Bridges–Adams regime, which included a sliding stage split in the middle with a 22-foot wing clearance on each side. Under the sliding stage were two massive lifts which between them could fill the entire space left by the sliding stage. There were two revolves in the Prompt and OP corners. Devine used the lot. Volpone's bedroom with its massive four-poster bed with a triptych as reredos slid out of view to make room for the arrival of the Senate coming up from the depths almost like a cinema organ, and houses spun round in the corners. The designer, Malcolm Pride, had framed the sets with a Venetian surround including St Mark's and gondolas. The treasure shrine was revealed when one of the gilded pineapples was twisted on the bedposts, and St Mark's Square slid into view as the bedroom disappeared, only to roll sideways to reveal the interior for the court scenes. As one reviewer put it, the stage did everything except sit up and beg! It was all visually very thrilling and made a great deal of sense. It recalled Inigo Jones and reminded us that in the masques at the Jacobean court the scenery was supposed to change before our very eyes, the mechanical marvels being part of the show. Jonson only opposed these mechanical marvels when they threatened to become more important than his words. So in this production the audience was in no danger of eye-starvation. But there were disadvantages. The production was long in spite of quite severe cutting, and the changes were noisy and not always reliable. On one night the lift stage was stopped in mid-descent, leaving Richardson in the top half of Volpone's bedroom; and on another occasion the audience were given the additional treat (during a power failure) of watching the sets cranked into position by huge hand-operated windlasses.

If Wolfit was often more of a lion than a fox, Richardson (possibly reacting against that interpretation) eliminated anything of that broad gusty humour that Wolfit saw in the character and which led him to cut as far as possible any passage that made Volpone either helpless or ludicrous. Richardson, in contrast, gave us a Volpone withdrawn and old, a weary aristocrat from whom Celia could scarcely be said to be in any danger. This seems to have been Richardson's decision. Irving Wardle recalls (in *The Theatres of George Devine*, 1978, p. 149) that during the 1952 season reviewers had decided that he was a 'mannered actor', and Devine worked hard to prevent this applying to *Volpone*. As Wardle relates, he constantly asked Richardson to speed up his delivery.

> Richardson listened with grave courtesy and invariably acquiesced. 'Absolutely', he would agree: 'of course, I do see'; only to revert to his old tempo when the scene came round again. 'In the end', says Quayle, 'Richardson did it his way.' In performance the actor always wins.

Wardle suggests that this was what often happened when Devine directed leading actors. He had authority 'but not the hypnotic dominance of directors like Guthrie . . .'. Devine always did his homework, rehearsals were well disciplined – Quayle described him as 'like a cabinet-maker, making a beautiful box' – but he could be overshadowed by outsize personalities. Any gusto in Richardson's performance was, as Harold Hobson remarked, concentrated in the make-up; this Volpone had 'a face and body of pasty deliquescence, much tricked out with finery. He looks like a corpse dressed up for a party' (*Sunday Times*, 20 July 1952). The slow delivery, drawing out every word to twice its natural length, meant that the voice, like the face, lacked anything of a foxy quality; and it was noted that, if Volpone looks a bit like a city gentleman, it takes more than a whispy ginger beard and oddly cut breeches to compensate for this. The mountebank scene (which Wolfit made sparkle and thunder) struck many as perfunctory, even lackadaisical. The low tension of this performance threw an unnatural weight on Celia and Mosca.

Celia, played by Siobhan McKenna, turned out to be an energetic young lady. The balcony scene showed her laughing gaily and frankly enjoying the show in the Square beneath her window, while her defence of virtue in the bedroom scene was so firm and strong-minded that Richardson's attack hardly looked likely to succeed. Hobson found this interpretation confusing. Celia emerged as two people: 'a forward young miss ogling strangers from her window', and 'a tough young creature noisily defending her virtue against all comers'. Hobson concluded that if she were the sort of girl who invites men into her bedroom and then screams for help, it was a good performance; if not, her view of the role was incomprehensible.

Where Wolfit had reduced the rule of Mosca, Richardson by reducing the energy of Volpone left the way open, dangerously, in performance as well as in the plot, for Mosca. Anthony Quayle's Mosca was, according to T. C. Worsley*, a 'delightful' creation – 'oily, sly and smooth, a Zeal-of-the-Lord Puritan with a touch of Uriah Heep, with drooping back, rubbing hands, meek knees and most insinuating voice – and consistently played from the inside' (*New Statesman*, 26 July, 1952). He reminded Hobson of 'marsh gas, and the bodies of putrefying fish', and ran away with the play as in the end he nearly runs away with Volpone's wealth. Such a performance enlarges a secondary character to large proportions, and this for many – apart from the mechanical antics of the stage – was the most striking feature of the production. Clothed in a shiny black costume (when not rubbing his hands together, he was massaging his legs), buzzing all the time and stressing his sibilants, Quayle looked like a large fly. When it was suggested to him that he was rather large for a fly, he replied that he would play Mosca as a bluebottle! But underneath this comic obsequiousness there was always a sense of menace. His moment of triumph in Act v showed him at a table the legs of which were carved and painted with black stockings and shoes

like his own, so that he really did appear at that moment to have
eight legs. And, of course, in Act v the roles *are* reversed. Where
the fly has buzzed around the fox, in the last act the fox has to
pursue Mosca who feigns deafness.

Harold Hosbon called his review: 'Why Volpone?' He began
by suggesting that there was no reason for Sir Ralph to play the
part and that Sir Ralph seemed to agree. T. C. Worsley found
the dominant note of the production 'antic' rather than 'acid'.
If power and fire seemed to have deserted Richardson, what
was left was his comic touch. The problem is that an actor of
Richardson's calibre knows the goodness of the human heart
and can do whatever is loving or kindly. The essence of
Richardson's acting always lay in his being a decent chap. The
essence of Volpone is that he is evil from the start, and
Richardson failed to suggest any sense of lust or sin. His craving
for Celia was never wholly believable. Mosca's description of
her in Act i produced in this Volpone only clownish surprise;
and throughout, Richardson's fox was not a monster but
rather, as Worsley put it, a 'crazy eccentric devising practical
jokes, which are played with a good-humoured self-
satisfaction, on some gulls who deserve nothing better'. A drily
comic performance, even if it lacks fire and gusto, could be
extremely satisfying, but Volpone is not a role that could be
completely captured by Richardson's special brand of quiet
comedy. His delight in knavery was beautifully suggested. He
was, as Ivor Brown put it in the *Observer* (20 July, 1952), 'every
inch a happy cozener but never the full-blooded lecher', and the
inadequacy of this presentation becomes clear as the violence of
the play begins to come through. It fails to harmonise with the
rapacity, the household pets, and ultimately with the scene in
which rape is threatened – where, as Worsley drily observed,
we had the curious spectacle of 'Sir Ralph . . . moaning on the
ground while Celia knelt over his prostrate body begging him to
let her go'.

Most reviewers, as usual, felt that the subplot ought to be
cut, though there was praise for Michael Hordern's Sir Politick
(out of Lewis Carroll and never boring) and Rosalind Atkin-
son's portrait Lady Would-be in the manner of a pantomime
dame.

In short, an interesting Volpone, well mounted and splen-

didly staged and strongly acted all round, but lacking the
crucial savage streak. Worsley suggested that the play had been
prettified to fit in with Sir Ralph's 'over-gentle handling' of the
main part. Volpone's genius, even for wickedness, should
excite us. Richardson never created that sense of excitement or
danger. This version made audiences laugh but, as *The Times*
reviewer put it, 'there is no terror in our laughter'.

11   TYRONE GUTHRIE'S OLD VIC PRODUCTION, 1968

The interesting thing about the National Theatre production of
1968 is that we remember it as Sir Tyrone Guthrie's *Volpone*
rather than as Colin Blakely's Volpone. It is a production that
is memorable because of what the director did rather than for
anything else.

One of the options open to a director – as well as the bare
stage, the Venetian setting or a modern location – is to stress
the animal fable that gives the play its shape. Anthony
Quayle's 'bluebottle' Mosca was a good example in the
Devine–Richardson *Volpone* of 1952; and before that, in the
Macowan–Wolfit production of 1938, there had been hints at
the animal: a russet-bearded Volpone was dressed in fox furs,
while Voltore and Corbaccio had the costume and mannerisms of birds. The Avocatori wore spectacles and looked like
owls; but, confusingly, Corvino was played like a bull, while
Mosca imitated a serpent. But it is probably this production of
Guthrie's in 1968 that has given the play its fullest treatment as
a beast fable.

Guthrie had staged *Volpone* in Cambridge in the late 1920s
(for the Marlowe Society there) and had directed it with great
success at Minneapolis in 1964. Of this American production
Henry Popkin* noted that the main impression was visual – in
the make-up, gait and, above all, the costumes designed by
Tanya Moiseiwitsch. Guthrie here retained most of the subplot, presenting us not merely with two simple-minded English
tourists who are trying to be super-subtle Venetians, but also
with characters who reinforce the idea that innocence is
ridiculous, even deplorable. He wrote in the programme note
that there are no virtuous characters in *Volpone* – which suggests

that Celia and Bonario are to be seen as too stupid to appear on any moral scale. This 1964 production had many excellent touches. For example, Volpone as Scoto climbs up to Celia's window only to meet Corvino who pushes the ladder away. Volpone falls backwards into the arms of his accomplices, who have to rush across the stage to catch him. Guthrie also elucidated the motivation of the last Act by making Volpone very drunk when begetting the idea of dying and making Mosca his heir (a reasonable use of v i). But in making the legacy-hunters so obviously figures of fun, Guthrie underlines the weakness of his interpretation.

The National Theatre production at the Old Vic was very much a duplicate of this earlier success. As its Volpone, Colin Blakely, remarks:

> [Guthrie] used the same props and costumes. In America it was obviously very lusty and broad; you have to make it lusty to make the Americans laugh. The English audience wanted something more subtle and friendly. Guthrie didn't do an awful lot of line analysis. He was a great one for 'Say as much as you can in one breath'; and dressing it up – which I think was probably wrong. He disguised Jonson. We'd never acted Jonson before, and we hadn't thought enough about him. We got it on, but that is all we did. It became beaky and all that; the words went out of the window. (*Gambit*, 6, no. 22, 1973, p. 15.)

Looking back, Blakely described the main thrust of the production as making it funny and warm:

> I remember thinking in rehearsals, 'The animal is what's inside the man but he's still a man. He's just called Volpone the Fox; so why do we give him a false nose? We just thought we had to; that was our bit to do. We tried to make it funnier.'

When Wolfit came on the stage and spoke the opening lines, it was not funny. Here, the audience thought, is a very serious and dangerous character. At the Old Vic, Blakely got a laugh at the opening line ('Good morning to the day; and, next, my gold') – which, as he admits, was what they were after. Ironically, while preparing for the role Blakely was filming with Wolfit (and with Leo McKern who had played Volpone at the Oxford Playhouse in 1966–67, directed by Frank Hauser).

Wolfit wrote him a note before the play opened but was discreetly silent afterwards.

This was a Volpone clad in red furs, emitting odd foxy yelps (practised from tapes of actual foxes), while Mosca wore a shiny black costume pinched in at the waistline and tight on the arms and legs. For the birds Tanya Moiseiwitsch had designed six-inch beaks, feather capes and gloves with long talons. Voltore was grim and broad-winged, while Corbaccio was a mass of rags and feathers. But there seemed to be no particular avian role for Corvino in this scheme. The vulture at least was a great success – Ronald Bryden* described Voltore as like 'a great bomber taking off'. Sir Politick and Lady Would-be became parrots (as scholarship had indicated); Graham Crowden's Sir Pol was splendid as a withered bird with 'slow winking eyes, leathery tongue clicking and whistling in a dry mouth, feet restlessly clawing at an invisible perch' (Alan Brien, *Sunday Telegraph*, 21 Jan., 1968). Martin Esslin, who saw the Politick Would-be couple as largely redundant characters, complimented Guthrie on making them 'objects of fascination and delight' since Crowden and Gabrielle Laye created such perfect upper-class boobies that the topical satire of Jonson's own time became satire for our time. But making them into parrots weakens the force of their names – would-be politicians – and encourages critics like Esslin to go on writing about the loose connection and redundant nature of the subplot.

Moreover a large question mark hangs over Guthrie's brilliant stage image of animality. As Robert MacDonald commented (*Scotsman*, 22 Jan., 1968), it is difficult to condemn a vulture for behaving like a vulture. The actors had been sent to Regent's Park Zoo to study animal behaviour and really had caught the movement and mannerisms of their appropriate bird or beast. But this resulted in altogether too much movement and twitching. In the longer run, the images are restrictive and distracting. Jonson gets his animal imagery in at the beginning and, having once got it planted in our minds, he lets it drop. Yet costumes and mannerisms once begun must continue to the end of the play. E. B. Partridge* noted that animal imagery 'all but ceases from the end of the first act until the beginning of the fourth. Jonson may have though that, once he started the comparisons working, he ought not to stress them lest the emphasis be taken from the human point of view' (*The Broken Compass*, p. 86). It is this human point of view which makes the play so 'implacable', to use Yeats's term.

Colin Blakely believed that he had failed with the role. When asked what the rewards of playing Volpone were, he replied frankly: 'None, because I failed. I didn't get it off the ground. It needs something huger than I was.' But his Volpone was very much in the tradition of gusty humour. According to Ronald Bryden (*Observer*, 21 Jan., 1968), Blakely brought to the part 'a fierce, grinning gusto complemented rather than handicapped by its superimposition on his rather stocky, squirearchical physique. As he springs bright-eyed and bare-foot from his reddish fur covers, he is both Reynard and his heavy, red-cheeked pursuer.' Guthrie, possibly helped by his Irish background, had turned the production into a marvellous fox hunt, getting coarse Englishness into the production under all the Venetian spectacle.

The animal imagery insisted upon a great deal of energetic business – something at which Guthrie always excelled. Volpone upon waking up washes himself in gold coins (which stick to his face and hands), feeding the odd coin, wafer-like, to a kneeling Mosca; and, using his bed like a trampoline, he bounces up and down at any mention of gold or plate. Mosca bounds into Volpone's lap and the birds bounce on the invalid's bed. Volpone bounces after Celia (looking like a small boy who has lost his favourite toy when his playfulness is frustrated by a noble but stupid Bonario). Henry Popkin* characterised the mood of Volpone's ménage as 'nearly innocent jollity' (*The Times*, 17 Jan., 1968), and this appears, for example, in the treatment of the household pets. Guthrie's prompt books refer to the dwarf, the eunuch and the hermaphrodite-fool as 'the children' or 'the kids', and they are in his production treated as Volpone's children. The Fox is fond of them, romping with them on his bed, giving them sweets and generally joining in their play: a view which accords with his words to them in Act v sc. xi.

But movement and jollity, if initially exciting, begin to pall when they are unremitting – and, indeed, may be said to distract the audience, in the wrong way, from the implacable nature of the play they are watching. Guthrie used movement to make a point. Thus, in Act I, his Volpone took immense risks in leaving his bed to roam about fetching sweets and offering them to Mosca. Corbaccio is written by Jonson as deaf but not blind, though his sight is not good and he may not notice everything that goes on in the bedchamber. But Volpone in this production did the same with the other characters, creating the impression that this was all just theatrical play, not behaviour contained within a play. For example, Corbaccio was encouraged to wander off into the audience. As at Minneapolis, the Scoto scene was spectacular. Volpone climbed up to Celia's balcony humming an aria from *Don Giovanni* (another dark comedy) and made his spectacular fall, after which the stage was cleared as if by magic. It certainly showed that Guthrie could handle a good crowd scene, but it moved the action forward very little. The chastity belt was firmly omitted. The seduction scene was carefully choreographed and turned into a romp (with some critics finding Gillian Barge's Celia too robust and too loud in her protestations). Ronald Bryden felt that Volpone's wooing of Celia was 'chopped up with comic skirmishings round the room and lascivious wrestling-holds among the pillows, forfeiting the cumulative incantatory force of the most superb poetic tirade outside Marlowe'. Esslin, on the other hand, in *Plays and Players* (March 1968), saw it as a 'horrifyingly realistic, terrifyingly suspenseful scene of rape and seduction' in which a grotesque figure in his night-shirt chases a lady who believed him to be on his death-bed round his bedroom – 'a corpse turned satyr'. They are both, of course, describing the same scene. What Bryden is asking for is the poetry.

All this physical movement is simply not what Jonson wanted. Volpone's belief is that Celia will yield to his verse, and force is his last, thwarted, resort. Wolfit made his move only at the end, and it was a slow pacing across the room which produced the right sense of horror. What Guthrie achieved in directing Blakely and Barge was nearer a romp in the dorm.

And having sustained a splendid busy jollity throughout the play, Guthrie is faced with the severity of the ending. In Minneapolis he tried out the idea of having the cast unite to sing a madrigal before the epilogue – which caused some confusion. At the Old Vic he dropped the epilogue altogether to emphasise what he called in his programme note the 'delicious sadism' of the conclusion. A senile court roared with laughter as each sentence was passed. But, as Ronald Bryden remarked, it is at the end of the play that Jonson gathers up all the strands for a final scene where an impersonal order takes over; by guying judges who, after all, dispense justice seasoned with wit and wisdom, Guthrie blurs the point. Esslin noted that the judges, as 'incarnations of senile imbecility', worked very well in the first courtroom scene where Volpone and his clients deceive them; but their stupidity in that scene makes it all the more difficult to take seriously the sudden access of wisdom in Act v.

Frank Wylie played Mosca with a Scots accent ('some repellant insect hatched in the Gorbals', according to Philip French in the *New Statesman*). But he was kept too busy dancing and darting around as a fly to have much breath for the verse. Blakely kept him company in this and seemed not to have mastered the requirements of speaking Jonson's poetry. Martin Esslin rejects the cliché that Guthrie always overloads his productions with tricks and gimmicks at the expense of the words, but some clichés have point to them because they are true. For Esslin, Volpone's running around the bedroom in pursuit of Celia and panting out the remarkable poetry 'not only enhanced the poetry, it became the very essence of the true magic of drama' – whatever that means. Jonson would have insisted that the words did the characterisation and that all this fancy dress and movement – both of which are in the character of Volpone – only served to disguise *Volpone*.

12 Paul Scofield: Peter Hall's National Theatre Production, 1977

The problems of any modern production of *Volpone* are, not surprisingly, the problems that have bedevilled the play since Jonson's own time: how the play should look and how far the scenery should be allowed to distract from the words; the character of Volpone and his relationship with Mosca; the serious ending of the play; how much of the subplot to retain; and how to present Celia and Bonario who, if minor characters, loom large in challenging the credibility of the production. The director must at all times recognise that he has to persuade audiences that, although they are not watching Shakespeare, they are watching a play by his most impressive rival. Wolfit's statement about the Macowan production is still very revealing. He noted that the 'bitter savagery of Jonson was stressed and the broad gusty humour which disarms the nastiness . . . was to some extent lacking', but it pleased 'a highly sophisticated audience and ran for six weeks'. Wolfit thought that a simpler version might be played to 'please audiences everywhere'.

A large institution like the National Theatre can afford to play Jonson any way it likes, and the 1977 production had a star-studded cast led by Paul Scofield. The director, Peter Hall, chose Renaissance costumes and an elegant set by John Bury. This *Volpone*, mounted at the Olivier theatre less than ten years after the Guthrie production for the National Theatre at the Old Vic, was not to be presented as a symbolic menagerie, with characters as zoological specimens, but rather as a play about men and women very much like you and me and capable, like us, of being silly or greedy.

The set was not going to create Venice – television can do that – but it sought rather to give us a suggestion of Venice: one far removed from the elaborate splendours of the Devine–Richardson production of 1952 but in its own way sumptuous. Three ceramic-tiled avenues radiated away into the blackness through pointed iron archways hung with swing-doors that could change from beaten gold to simple white. When the screens which formed a semi-circle around the playing area opened at the beginning of the play, there was a physical sense of gold dominating the stage; and the archways and marble floors served as Volpone's bedroom, the streets of Venice or the courtroom. Whether this slight symmetrical set coped with the immensity of the Olivier theatre is open to question – as, indeed, is the sense of staging so claustrophobic a play on an arena stage. Ned Chaillet (*Plays and Players*, June 1977) thought it did, and Irving Wardle described it as the best use yet made of the Olivier stage (but he must have overlooked, or not seen, Peter Hall's production of *Tamburlaine* in that same theatre, in the previous year). For some, however, the set seemed dwarfed in the vastness of the building; and while the screens worked very well to suggest doors, walls and closets, they are rather too delicate to contain the extravagant furniture and props. What such a set did was to facilitate speed. Guthrie, by adding business, had slowed down the play; and Malcolm Pride's rich Venetian setting for the 1952 production, while it may have been a stage-mechanic's dream, must have been a producer's nightmare. Peter Hall's production moved at speed from the first moment, when Scofield came through the centre doors with his exuberant, 'Good morning to the day . . .'.

Before this happened, however, Hall had had the interesting idea of getting Sir John Gielgud (his Sir Politick) to recite the prologue from a corner of the auditorium, wearing a lounge-suit. The lights then went up as Scofield entered, swathed in red brocade, to hail the day and the proceeds of his past deceits. Deirdre Clancy's costumes only hinted at the animal world: Volpone's sleek greying hair was still a bit red on top, while Sir Politick wore coloured feathers in his cap. This allowed the play to be obviously about people and the audience were not encouraged to feel that they were watching predators so exaggerated and unhuman that any resemblance to life or themselves was purely coincidental.

Scofield's Volpone had panache. It was an aristocratic performance, the Scofield walk being used to good effect and full value given to the words. The criticism that he looked too good for the part (and he was certainly more leonine than vulpine), that there should be some physical repulsiveness to match the hypocrisy, misses the point. But it also makes one. It is a point of a different order from that levelled against Richardson, whose decency could only be disguised as comic shrewdness. Scofield gave us a magnifico of Venice, a grandee who was rather languid until he decided to take a role in the action – when, as in the Scoto scene, his energy was tremen-dous. But there was no hint of vulgarity in his performance, much less the earthiness which both Wolfit and Blakely managed to get. Scofield's Volpone was never less than dignified, a man whose powers were fuelled by greed, whose passion is not appeased by pleasure but only by novelty. This Volpone could switch immediately from his handsome private self to the decrepit invalid in a breathtaking way, which lent weight to his obvious conviction that simple transformation from corpse to lover would be enough to woo and win Celia. His sonorous voice gave weight to the verse. Peter Hall has always insisted on the correct delivery of verse, and here was an actor who could say the words, shaping his voice around them, the grand 'poetic' voice collapsing into the decrepit voice all wheezes and coughs in a marvellous way. He sang the song to Celia unaccompanied in a strong baritone voice (to music composed by Harrison Birtwhistle) – few, if any, Volpones have managed that before – and his handling of the verse–arias in the seduction episodes led John Elsom (*Listener*, 5 May 1977) to write of 'delicate sensuality' (though with the foolish comment that the girl was stupid to refuse). Scofield even shifted tone inside the lines so that the sense of 'quick Negro' to 'cold Russian' [III vii 232] was matched by a shift from warmth to ice in the voice. Celia was wooed with a display of gold and a display of learning, the opening speech capturing that elegant *self-admiring* tone which gradually gave way to a quieter, more chilling note until he has to resort to force. Scofield also caught that sense of heroic pride which makes the final self-exposure both believable and exciting. At the end he received the judgment of the Court with suitable disdain.

A lordly figure in fox-red robes, then, but lacking some of the earthiness and gusto. Robert Cushman (*Observer*, 1 May 1977) dubbed him the aesthete Fox but recalled that Wolfit's Volpone was greasier and dustier. Scofield, in John Bury's restrained set, gave a classical performance of the play which Jonson would have liked but something was missing: the madness that drives all these people whom Jonson created not like you and me but as monsters. John Barber summed it up in the *Daily Telegraph* (27 April 1977):

> What I missed was the manic Jonsonian tension, the massive voltage in man's bitter trouncing of human greed and pettiness. Perhaps the thing looked too pretty. Perhaps the laughter was too good-tempered, the sensuality too polite. Scofield himself too noble a figure. Or perhaps the director is too amiable a man.

Mosca was played by Ben Kingsley. Clad in black lace he made the perfect fly; perhaps too perfect. Michael Billington saw him as Iago-like with a 'black habit, pale face and an unknowable

heart', a supreme practical joker (*Guardian*, 27 April 1977). His
voice is lighter than Scofield's, and his movements were quicker
so that he darted about the stage ceaselessly: the expert hustler
who was compared by John Elsom with the manipulator of
international business deals – talking 'as if on three or four
phones at once and blaming the switchboard for momentary
delays' (*Listener*, 5 May 1977). As such he became a recognis-
ably modern figure. (*Time* magazine called him 'the unctuous
image of the Madison Avenue PR man', which is fair enough
since Volpone is a kind of asset stripper who prays on ailing
people rather than ailing firms.) But again there was something
missing: the eccentric flight of a Mosca possessed, the self-
admiring rascal who loves the game and meets every challenge
as it comes. Kingsley's Mosca did not live in danger of being
found out, of being at his wit's end, aware that the great empire
he is creating is only a house of cards that could collapse at any
moment. He also played the part as if he included himself in his
disgust with the world. This made an excellent foil for Scofield's
dispassionate Volpone but, as John Peter suggested, it was an
actor's opinion of Mosca rather than the fly itself. It was a
clever performance in the wrong way.

Volpone's household had a kind of sober realism about it,
too. Nano was played by David Rappaport who is about
three-feet tall and described by Peter Hall in his Diary (22
February 1977) as 'a perfectly normal, joyous dwarf . . .
disturbing yet utterly charming and comic'. Imogen Claire in
platform boots played the hermaphrodite-fool wearing a beard
with her breasts bared. This, of course, is a freedom in the
theatre that would have surprised Wolfit (and his provincial
audiences too). A plump counter-tenor appeared as Castrone,
completing a trio of characters that were odd in an ordinary
sort of way. They were only faintly disturbing. The same sane
approach was extended to the dupes. These were less birds of
prey than human beings who were venal and ambitious. They
were often funny – Corbaccio was forever trying to make his
exit through closed doors – but Paul Rogers gave Voltore little
of his legal slipperiness, while Michael Medwin's Corvino was,
with some justification, described by one critic as 'wet and
droopy'. Certainly he never began to probe the brutality of his
jealousy. What was missing, again, was what Michael Billing-

ton called 'the single-mindness of overpowering financial lust' (*Guardian*, 27 April 1977).

Celia and Bonario were, perhaps inevitably, presented as young fools. It was, however, a good idea to cast Warren Clarke, who is a stocky actor, in the role of Bonario since he looks and acts entirely unlike the traditional romantic young hero. Both were smug in their reliance on justice and truth upheld by religion, and this smugness produced easy laughter. Jonson would not, in his complex morality, have dismissed the case for religion quite so lightly as modern audiences were encouraged to do here. They took the invitation liberally.

The text, too, had been smoothed out, yet not – as Bernard Levin complained – simply 'to make it easier for fools', but (again) to make it immediately accessible, comfortable. Thus, one of Gielgud's funniest remarks as Sir Politick is not in Jonson's text. It is easy to be patronising about changes to the text (as I suspect Levin was being). Certainly it is in the subplot that a racy colloquial spirit prevails, suitable to English tourists; yet this may have become more 'dated' than the poetry of Volpone. Jonson's purpose was to teach through entertainment, and no director (however scholarly) can require his audience to study a text thoroughly before visiting the theatre. Peter Hall did not make textual changes negligently. He records his admiration for Jonson's text in his Diary (1 January 1977), finding it more exciting in many ways than Shakespeare: 'more intellectual, more conscious, less instinctive, less naturally mellifluous; always stimulating'. But by 12 April he is finding the play much too long (three hours and more, not counting intervals). It is a familiar problem, as is that raised in his next remark: 'I don't know where to cut'. On the next day he is expressing the fear that, if he butchers the text too much, 'we . . . shall not be doing Jonson but a farce'. The textual changes were not excessive – indeed, Gielgud's funny remark mentioned above was simply an updating, and possibly more amusing than Jonson's original![1]

In short, this was an entertaining production (though not especially funny), with little sense of corruption, madness,

---

1. The phrase devised for Gielgud's Sir Politick, 'a thing for tavern talk', is a neat way of putting Jonson's 'talk for ordinaries' [v iv 84].

possession or even eccentricity – though the subplot, at least, provided a dash of this quality.

Peter Hall clearly recognised the symmetry of the two plots and played it fittingly in John Bury's symmetrical set. Oddly enough, however, there was no strong sense of the subplot's being connected in any thematic way with the main plot. This was possibly because the subplot had its own eccentric thrust with a classic performance by Sir John Gielgud, who made Sir Politick Would-be real, credible and recognisable to a modern audience without straying too far from Jonson's portrayal. As has been mentioned, Gielgud appeared at first in a lounge suit to recite the Prologue. He was then transformed into Sir Politick, in plus fours, feathered beret (golf cap?), carrying a camp stool and a tourist's shoulder-bag in which he was forever searching for this or that secret document. It was endearing, and it underlines what was happening. Here was one of the great actors of our time, famous for classic roles, turning in a cameo character part. Gielgud's Politick was officious, thick *but* kindly. Benedict Nightingale saw him as a character 'on day-release from a P. G. Wodehouse short story, forever inventing explanations for Venetian behaviour, finding spies and plots everywhere, and lecturing Peregrine on correct behaviour with that upper-class assurance that addresses you at length without ever speaking to you'. Gielgud captured precisely the fantasist in a real world while Volpone was, of course, the realist in the fantasy world of his clients.

Elizabeth Spriggs played Lady Would-be as a woman aware that she is boring but also aware that that is all she is. Rouged heavily on each cheek (and sunburned on her nose), she had a loud high voice, rather frayed red hair (which connected her with the Fox) and an inexorable manner. We shared Volpone's relief when Mosca got rid of her by hinting that Sir Politick was up to no good in a gondola on the way to the Rialto (an idea that Gielgud's performance had made quite unbelievable). With her buck teeth, her loquacity and her coyness she was all too familiar and real, and when she borrowed Volpone's dwarf the sight of this couple brought the house down.

Volpone is not only evil: he is endlessly beguiling. This was a beguiling production, but the darker sense was missing. It is significant that one does not particularly remember the ending.

The play and its characters seemed to crumble away. Eric Bentley maintains that there is always a tension in Jonson's plays between the author's conscious (and highly proper) ideas and his deep sense of chaos, and argues that this tension is more productive than either the ideas or the sense of chaos alone would produce. In *Volpone*, he suggests, there are no characters that we can like (we cannot after all *like* Celia or Bonario):

> and everyone is sick, not just to the point where he becomes believable, but far beyond it – to the point where you are tempted to disbelieve. Ben Jonson's characters are 'far out'. His world is a madhouse.   (*The Life of the Drama*, 1965, p. 269.)

Splendid though this production was, that dimension – the implacable element in Jonson's play – was missing. At least, initially. Peter Hall notes in his diary (23 September 1977) that the production got more ruthless:

> I think the sadistic thug in *Volpone*, the utterly selfish fascist, must in the end come out. We never in rehearsal got the scenes right that should show the cruel streak. They weren't cruel enough. At last both Paul and Ben have the predators' pleasure in total destruction.

So much so that Michael Medwin (Corvino) was startled to find them being so horrid to him, and wondered whether it was personal!

13   POSTSCRIPT: BILL ALEXANDER'S PRODUCTION, THE OTHER PLACE, 1983

The Other Place at Stratford-upon-Avon is a wooden shed with a floor and galleries and complete flexibility for staging. *Volpone*, because of the dominance of the bed, requires end-on staging. So, in Bill Alexander's production of 1983, the whole back wall of the acting area was timbered with black Jacobean panelling; this provided cupboards, windows, doors and small peepholes for Voltore and Volpone. In the centre of the floor was a small platform which, when covered with furs, served as Volpone's bed (with cupboards that held his props and costumes), and could be changed into a stage for Scoto or a dais for the judges (here reduced to two) or for Sir Politick's tortoise. When in bed

Volpone was swathed in fox furs, but Richard Griffith's shape precluded any particular reference to animals. The three clients wore collars and trimmings of black feathers. Music (composed by Guy Woolfenden) was played from the galleries on either side, producing an 'antiphonal' effect similar to that in St Mark's basilica, but otherwise the only suggestions of Venice came from the text.

This simple set managed, however, to be decidedly opulent in its use. When Richard Griffith entered in a blaze of light from the back to greet the morning and his gold, Mosca (Miles Anderson) rushed around opening cupboards which glowed with treasures and teemed with legal documents. This profusion Volpone blessed with wine in a solemn manner – an effect undercut when he accidentally sprinkled Mosca who was standing by peeling an orange for Volpone's breakfast.

Nano was accompanied by a punk girl with a codpiece and a sad-looking, bald eunuch. They clearly loved Volpone, romping on his bed and presenting the masque to him as he lolled on cushions on the floor puffing at a hookah. The production kept these three characters firmly in view even when the text only refers to them (e.g., they were present at the wooing of Celia). The gulls were received and deceived (with the aid of make-up, and a fart cushion that kept them at a distance from Volpone!). Mosca's mention of Celia led to Volpone's petulant demand that he must see her, immediately.

Where the dwarf gabbled the lines of the masque (which are thematically resonant), Scoto–Volpone made heavy weather of his market-place spiel. Richard Griffith made every word clear, either to ensure that we saw it was rubbish or to convey the idea that it was not at the forefront of Volpone's mind. He was waiting for the only closed window to open (and reveal Celia), and when it did he missed it. A good effect, but got at a high price since we lost Volpone's zest for acting and the scene seemed overlong. It was brought to an end by the arrival of Corvino (John Dicks) carrying a canvas bag. This contained a chastity belt, clearly bought on the way home by a husband alarmed at Mosca's suggestions in Act I. It became an amusing embarrassment (he had nowhere to put it down) as he talked with Mosca.

Celia was presented by Julie Peasgood as a mixture of pliant, even loving wife (when Corvino was sentenced in Act v she moved across the stage to stand by his side) and religious hysteric. When offered to Volpone she held on to anything she could (such as the seats at the edge of the stage) and lay flat on the floor, rigid, until Mosca carried her smilingly to the bed. Volpone sang to her (just). But the main effect of the wooing scene was the presence at the upper windows of the dwarf, fool and eunuch who sprinkled the couple with rose petals! Bonario (Nigel Cooke) was introduced as a bookish young man wearing spectacles and a large, incongruous sword (which fortunately he did not have to wear in the courtroom scenes). He was the sort of fool, who having rescued Celia, took her out by the wrong door and so had to re-enter and cross the stage with her. During the courtroom scenes they remained smug and reliant on heaven and its justice, which had little chance before the onslaught of Voltore (Henry Goodman). This was a chilling performance as the predatory lawyer stripped off a few garments, warming to his task, and it prepared us for the madness of Corvino and Voltore in the final scene: obsession and possession indeed, reminding us that the real villains of the piece are the bourgeois Venetians.

The subplot was largely retained (and the audience loved it), but it was taken at a very slow pace and not really connected to the main plot. Perhaps Jonson was too clever here and the subplot does not connect – in the theatre, at any rate. The tortoise scene, however, was a triumph. When Sir Politick said he had an engine, indeed he had. Pulling a lever at the side of the stage, Bruce Alexander brought down from the ceiling a large tortoise shell. Gemma Jones's Lady Would-be was both too beautiful and too elegant (though in moments of excitement her vowels slipping into unladylike East End diction). But at least she recognised that her chatter is just chatter and took it at a pace the other actors could well imitate.

Miles Anderson's Mosca wore rusty black satin (which could well have been black leather) and a black ear-stud, and his hair was greased so that it shone like the wings of a fly; he looked as if he would mug you on any subway. But he played the role as a man coming to the end of his tether rather than as one rejoicing in living at the end of his wits. A programme note explained the events of the day by suggesting that, after three years of success,

Volpone's and Mosca's 'incompatibilities of class and temperament' bring about discovery and fall. This is one way of
'explaining' the unities and the catastrophe, but it is not really
in the text. Mosca, when asked to produce Celia, leaned against
the wall as if to ask for time to think; and his claim that getting
Volpone off the rape charge *must* be their masterpiece [v ii 13]
seemed to express the hope that they could rest now. Certainly,
when Volpone rose to this challenge and proposed the final
plot, Mosca was stopped in his tracks, literally, and it took time
for the implications to sink in. His soliloquy [III i] was curiously
underplayed – like Volpone's epilogue (and in the same
spotlight).

The production attempted to mitigate the ending's harshness by having one of the judges howl with laughter as each
sentence was pronounced, but this worked no better here than
in the Guthrie production of 1968. Nor was it necessary. The
madness of the courtroom scene made the judgement welcome.

Few critics seemed worried about the verse speaking.
Richard Griffith's Volpone is certainly one for the books – the
first fat Volpone? Wonderful in some effects – particularly
when he was lying in bed, like some large baby watching the
antics of the world about him – yet he lacked the contrast
between invalid and magnifico. As Francis King observed
(*Sunday Telegraph*, 9 Oct. 1983), instead of turning into a man
agile of mind and body he merely suggested 'that the corpulent
invalid has taken a temporary turn for the better'. Griffith
never caught the sensual poetic Renaissance monster. John
Barber (*Daily Telegraph*, 7 Oct. 1983) saw him as 'an elephan-
tine Buddha a-shake with a palsy'; and, while Michael
Billington and others found him splendid, Irving Wardle
seemed nearer the truth when he wrote (*The Times*, 7th Oct.
1983) that Griffiths is a comic actor who 'excels in discomfiture'
but is hardly one of natures's foxes: 'What is missing in the
performance is sheer appetite. Like many bulky actors, Mr
Griffiths lacks sensuality . . .'. In a play about shape-changing
his shape remained unchangeable; and his voice had the same
quality too. When he brought in a 'poetic' touch it sounded
false. Volpone, moreover, is an athlete's role, and here was a
perpetually sweaty, breathless Volpone.

In a glowing review of the production, Richard Edmonds

(*Birmingham Post*, 6 Oct. 1983) claimed that Jacobean satire was brought into the realms of bedroom farce. That is always the danger but it is one that the director, Bill Alexander, resisted. It was a long evening (clumsy cutting was offset by slow pacing) but it was impressive. Although one missed in Volpone and Mosca the element of daring energy, many of the details – fart cushion, Peregrine pinned to the ground by Lady Would-be, the lever-operated tortoise shell – made for a richly comic entertainment. Yet a murderous Mosca (one sees why the household clung to Volpone in his downfall – life with Master Mosca would not be fun) and the madness of Voltore and Corvino ensured that this was no farce, only a mad world momentarily checked by a stupid justice and the liberating lines of an epilogue.

READING LIST

Robert Gale Noyes, *Ben Jonson on the English Stage: 1660–1776* (1935) covers seven plays; ch. 1 deals with the main currents of criticism, ch. 2 looks specifically at *Volpone*. R. B. Parker, 'Volpone in Performance: 1921–1972', *Renaissance Drama*, n.s. IX (1978), pp. 147–73, does the same for the modern period, and is complemented by ch. 4 in Michael Scott, *Renaissance Drama and a Modern Audience* (1982). What often happened to the play in the theatre is discussed by David McPherson, 'Rough Beast into Tame Fox', *Studies in the Literary Imagination*, VI, no. 1 (1973), pp. 77–84. R. B. Parker's study of Wolfit – 'Wolfit's Fox: An Interpretation of *Volpone*', *Univ. of Toronto Q.*, XLV, no. 3 (1976), pp. 200–20 – draws on the BBC film version, the prompt books, other material from Wolfit's scrapbooks and in the Victoria and Albert Museum, and discussions with Lady Wolfit, Michael Macowan, Ronald Harwood and John Mayes. (It gives detail to my own dim, if powerful, recollections.) For some idea of what Wolfit and his context were like (though its author is at pains to deny that 'Sir' is Wolfit), I would suggest Ronald Harwood's *The Dresser* (1980) – from which the 1984 film of the same title derives.

The obvious start for a study of the text is the Casebook edited by Jonas A. Barish (1972), which reproduces his article of 1953, 'The Double Plot in *Volpone*', among other good things. Barish also edited the 'Twentieth Century Views' collection on Jonson (1963), which includes T. S. Eliot's essay on Jonson of 1919. Eliot's brilliant and influential essay can also be found in his *The Sacred Wood* (1920) and in his *Selected Essays* (1932 and subsequent editions); and it is excerpted in the Casebook on the play. An interesting discussion of Jonson's plays and their economic background is given in L. C. Knights, *Drama and the Age of Jonson* (1937). Critical surveys of the dramatist's whole work which usefully discuss *Volpone* are: John J. Enck, *Jonson and the Comic Truth* (1957), ch. 6; and Edward B. Partridge, *The Broken Compass* (1958), ch. 5. Warmly recommended is Richard Dutton, *Ben Jonson: To the First Folio* (1983) and Anne Barton, *Ben Jonson: Dramatist* (1984), particularly chs 1–4.

INDEX OF NAMES